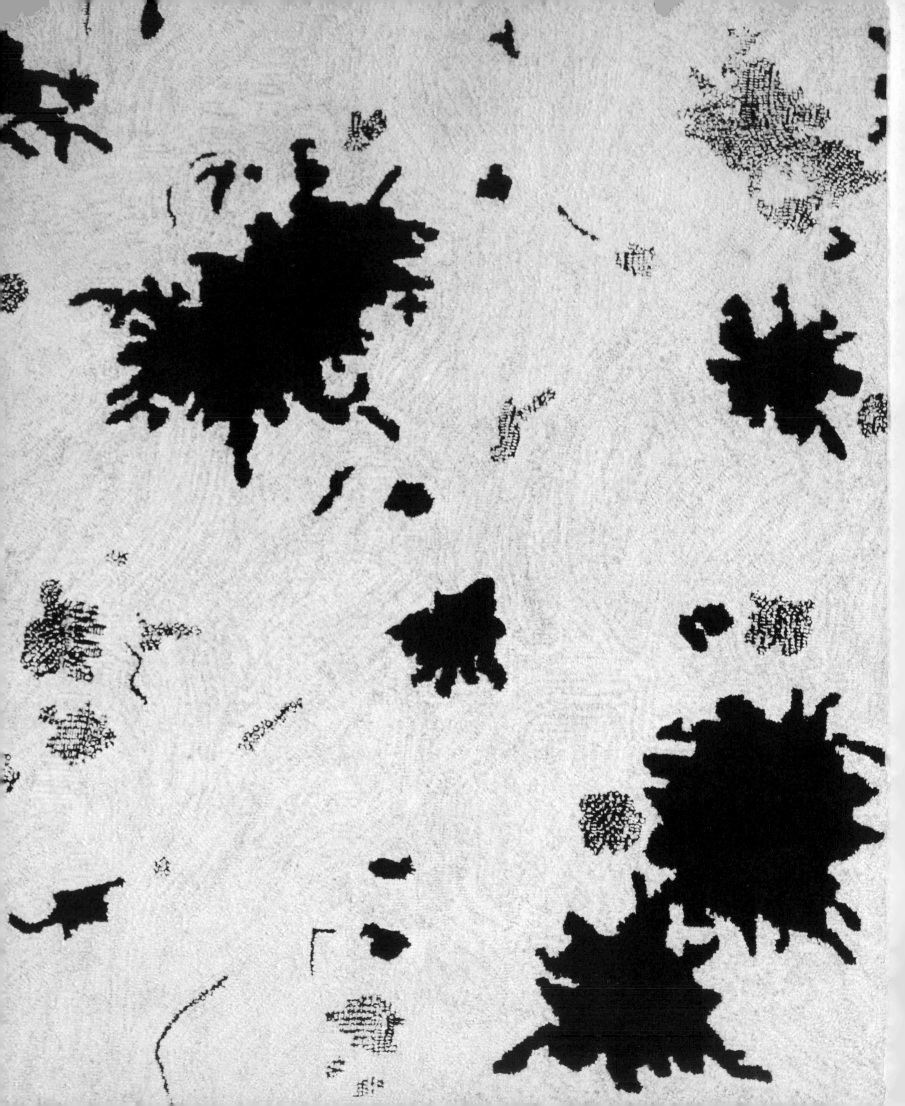

Make It
Fabulous

Make It Fabulous The Architecture and Designs of William T. Georgis

Edited and with essays by Donald Albrecht and Natalie Shivers

Principal photography by T. Whitney Cox

THE MONACELLI PRESS

To the memory of my mother, Mitzie Georgis,
who encouraged me to shoot my arrow high,
and to Richard D. Marshall, who has always
believed in me

FRONTISPIECE
Apartment, 2008: Rosewood-paneled library with view
toward adjacent dining room with Olafur Eliasson's hanging
light sculpture *Colour Globe*

Library of Congress Cataloging-in-Publication Data
Make it fabulous : the architecture and designs of William
T. Georgis / edited and with essays by Donald Albrecht and
Natalie Shivers ; principal photography by T. Whitney Cox.
pages cm
ISBN 978-1-58093-331-5 (hardback)
1. Georgis, William T., 1958– —Themes, motives.
2. Architecture, Domestic—United States.
3. Interior decoration—United States.
I. Albrecht, Donald. II. Shivers, Natalie W. (Natalie Wilkins).
III. Georgis, William T., 1958– Works. Selections.
NA737.G465A4   2013
728.092—dc232012048192

www.monacellipress.com

10 9 8 7 6 5 4 3 2 1
First edition

Designed by Pure+Applied | pureandapplied.com

Printed in China

Contents

Finding a Unique Voice

Donald Albrecht and Natalie Shivers

A vertiginous glass addition to a neo-Georgian townhouse, a hall of smoked mirrors used as a dining room, Japanese tea papers gilding a living room ceiling, closets concealed by a seventeenth-century Coromandel screen, a disco ball spinning above an ancient Roman torso, tables of anthracite coal and a black rabbit rug in a Manhattan library, a powder room with bullet-riddled mirrored walls: these are just a few of the signatures of William T. Georgis. His work is characterized by provocative juxtapositions of elements from different eras, opulent and surprising materials, and an extraordinary level of care and craft. The effect is never dull, always fabulous.

In mixing historic and contemporary models to create a unique aesthetic, Georgis continues a time-honored practice of working within traditions and precedents, interpreting and transforming them to make something new and modern. While eighteenth-century aristocracy in France adapted ancient classicism into a distinctly French aesthetic, it was during the mid-twentieth century that designers like England's Edwin Lutyens, New York's Dorothy Draper, and Hollywood's Billy Haines created architecture and interiors that set the stage for

OPPOSITE
Georgis-Marshall Residence, "the Akropolis," La Jolla, 2011: Living room with reflection of a nineteenth-century painting of Greek ruins in Agrigento, a reference to both the house's terrain and namesake

Georgis's work more than half a century later. The seminal interwar work of these architects and interior designers updated staid traditions with a vibrant sense of color, distortion of scale, open plans and blank walls, and contemporary forms derived from historic models. These designers were also intent on creating their own ensembles of architecture, interiors, and decoration. While these are themes that characterize Georgis's work, the result is his own distinctive aesthetic.

The path to the architect's current practice was formed by a wide range of experiences and influences. As a young child in Oak Park, Illinois, where he was born in 1958, Georgis became enamored of architecture early. He was attracted to the "unique voice" of Frank Lloyd Wright's houses among the suburb's more traditionally designed residences. Georgis gave tours of these houses while in high school, which provided a chance to study in detail Wright's *Gesamtkunstwerks*—masterful integrations of architecture, interior design, decoration, and landscape. Another strong influence from his childhood was the Thorne Miniature Rooms at the Art Institute of Chicago; these introduced Georgis to the history of decorative arts and taught him how to use decoration to create stage sets for people's lives. Also formative for Georgis were the elegant houses of David Adler in the city's North Shore suburbs. Even then, he enjoyed the concept of grand houses that create continuity between a European past and an American future.

French Library of the Modern Period, 1930s, *Thorne Miniature Rooms, Art Institute of Chicago, c. 1937*

Georgis attended the Illinois Institute of Technology, a school designed by and following the precepts of German Bauhaus master Ludwig Mies van der Rohe, for one semester. There he acquired an appreciation of Mies's work: the Barcelona Pavilion and the Farnsworth House, according to Georgis, are "tattooed" on his brain. At IIT, Georgis studied Mies's concepts of architectural purity and focused on construction, detail, and craft. He continued his studies at Stanford University in California, graduating in 1980 with a degree in art history. At Stanford Georgis gained a broad liberal arts education and learned watercolor techniques, which he used to create renderings for competition entries in his early career. The young designer also learned the value of history as a source, a view that was largely absent from his IIT education.

For his masters degree in architecture, he turned to Princeton University, where the curriculum, under the influence of Michael Graves, was grounded in historical precedent and focused on Beaux-Arts principles of planning and issues of context and modernity. In his work today, Georgis adheres to the Beaux-Arts practice of starting a project with a parti, or architectural concept, and creating floor plans with strong formal relationships between spaces. And he continues to explore strategies for dealing with context—historic, geographic, architectural, cultural, personal.

After graduating from Princeton, Georgis sought positions with architects who integrated

Cabris Room, Wrightsman Galleries, Metropolitan Museum of Art, New York: Gallery devoted to the decorative arts of seventeenth- and eighteenth-century France

architectural history into contemporary practice, working briefly with Robert Venturi in Philadelphia and for almost a decade with Robert A. M. Stern in New York. Georgis credits Stern with his professional education; at the office, which grew from around fifteen employees when he started in 1983 to one-hundred-plus when he left, he found a collaborative environment with an enormous architectural library at its center. Using his watercolor skills, he worked on many competitions, including the winning design for the neocolonial Norman Rockwell Museum in Stockbridge, Massachusetts, which he guided through construction. Georgis also collaborated on the design of large private houses and their interior furnishings and developed licensed products: office furniture for HBF, linens and sheets for Martex, and tableware for Swid Powell.

Georgis saw Stern's office as a model for his own practice in its integration of architecture and interior design. Stern's interest in research and his process of appropriating and building on history also proved highly influential on Georgis's later work. Stern notes of Georgis's time in the office that he himself was developing an architectural strategy of "creative recollection," moving toward a more scholarly approach to history and honing his program of "recuperation of the past in order to meet the expectations of the present." Stern imparted to his staff a regard for architecture as part of a visual continuum. Stern and Georgis, however, differ in their approaches and their sources. While Stern sees his buildings as extensions of history, drawing

Tugendhat House, Brno, Czech Republic, 1930: Designed by Mies van der Rohe

Lever House, New York, 2001: Lobby

primarily on American and Western European sources, Georgis's approach to the past varies widely and his palette includes popular culture, the architectural traditions of diverse countries and times, and decorative and fine arts—or, as he says, "all eras, all cultures—no limits."

This period also fostered Georgis's interest in the transgressive and the subversive, themes that would recur in his designs after he left the Stern office. Georgis says, "It was a kind of unbridled time: the tail end of the seventies—Studio 54 and the Saint—and then in the eighties it was the Palladium and Area. I think people had a good time." Much of Georgis's work not only incorporates references to 1970s culture and design but pushes boundaries—and buttons. One client describes his work as "daring," noting that "Bill wants to surprise, to slightly shock, to severely challenge the establishment."

Another signature theme that emerged from this period is the incorporation of art into Georgis's projects. For this he credits his partner, art curator and adviser Richard D. Marshall, whom he met in 1989. Marshall, at that time a curator at the Whitney Museum of American Art, introduced Georgis to the world of contemporary art. Marshall also introduced Georgis to his first clients, South American art collectors, whose commission for an apartment renovation in the Carlyle Hotel launched the architect's independent practice. Since then Marshall and Georgis have collaborated on many projects, with Marshall often advising Georgis's clients on starting, expanding, and/or installing their collections and assisting with the selection and direction of artists for site-specific works.

Today, working out of a Manhattan townhouse that serves as his office and home, Georgis focuses primarily on residential projects, both new construction and custom renovations, although he has designed office interiors and cultural facilities, including the Tiffany & Co. Foundation Gallery at the Museum of the City of New York. His commercial projects, most commissioned by his residential clients—the Lever House public spaces, the Gramercy Park Hotel, Chinatown Brasserie—are primarily renovations that call for him to reimagine existing spaces and structures. "In New York there is a limited market for new building. At the same time, while working for Robert Stern, I had the practical experience of designing interiors and furnishings, which I had loved as a child," Georgis says. His early independent projects were interior renovations, and he grew to find inspiration in the challenges and opportunities offered by working within existing contexts. Recognizing analogies between the New York and Italian scenes, Georgis cites the work of Italian architect Carlo Scarpa, who had "a great career within the constraints of renovation, creating rich dialogues between historic and contemporary design."

With a staff of twelve architects and interior designers, Georgis is committed to a hybrid practice that merges architecture, interior design, and decoration. His interest in creating holistically deters him from taking on a decorating job without also designing the architecture—or vice versa. His

Apartment, 2008: Music room with Jeff Zimmerman's Drop lamps and George Condo's bronze portrait bust

Residence, 2009: Living room with wicker-and-light-bulb Transcloud sculpture designed for the space by the Brazilian Campana brothers

furnishing designs he considers distillations of his architecture and interior design—there is a seamless relationship between all parts of his projects. Georgis is conscious of the traditional split between the professions of architect and decorator. Yet, he notes, "There are so many really great architectural spaces that are not comfortably decorated and end up being difficult to live in. So I like to think that I bring an architect's sensibility to the decoration, reinforcing or working against the architectural envelope and having the decorating somehow participate as a positive player in the conversation. Unlike many architects, I am proud to decorate."

Georgis traces his aesthetic trajectory from historicism while at Stern's office to modernism when he started his own practice and then back again to an appreciation of history: "I've always loved architecture from all periods, but after leaving Robert Stern's, I reacted to his historicism and went to the opposite extreme. My work became much more modern, even though the references were to mid-twentieth-century modernism. As time progresses, I'm swinging back to an appreciation of old things, old details." In his first independent projects, Georgis's strategy was to challenge the context, telling his clients, "You're in a prewar building, so let's fight it, let's do something different, let's break out of the box." But now Georgis acknowledges that he has "a further appreciation of historicism." He starts the design of all projects—once he has familiarized himself with the physical context and interviewed his clients about their program—with historical research. Georgis's studies produce precedent images of interiors, buildings, and details for his projects. Often these may seem unrelated— he may look at a rococo palace for the renovation of a log cabin, for instance—yet he uses them to weave narratives for the creation of highly customized settings for his clients' lives.

Georgis's aesthetic has evolved into one based on strong formal plans of discrete but linked rooms, rather than the open plans of his earlier work, and on a dense juxtaposition of materials, finishes, and artifacts from different cultures and eras. "My work," Georgis says, "is becoming more layered and more inclusive of decorative arts from other periods, and also more responsive to context." His design method, while highly disciplined and rigorously detailed, involves a certain amount of improvisation. He develops the parti and plan, simultaneously considering the concepts for architecture and furniture. At the same time, he begins to shop for furnishings, a process Georgis likens to playing pinball or chess, where each move sets up other moves: "An interesting thing happens when you start shopping—serendipity kicks in. So you might find a piece that completely throws the concept off or knocks it in another direction or adds another layer, another cultural reference."

When discussing his primary sources, Georgis cites a panoramic range of eras and cultures. He turns often to seventeenth- and eighteenth-century France, when designers made Italian Renaissance precedents their own, working within and transforming the

Paul Rudolph Apartment, New York, 1967–77: Designed by Rudolph

Georgis-Marshall Residence, La Jolla, 2011: Powder room with bullet-riddled mirrors and Japanese woodblock prints

classical tradition. This was also an era when patrons commissioned works from the greatest architectural and artistic talent of the day, placing a high premium on craft and quality. The Metropolitan Museum of Art's Wrightsman Galleries, which contain masterpieces of French decorative arts of this period, have served as valuable research resources for Georgis. America's Gilded Age interiors, which he describes as "a heady mix of Renaissance, Gothic Revival, contemporary furnishings, and fine art," also provide inspiration. More recent precedents include the work of Mies van der Rohe and American architect Paul Rudolph: Mies tempered his rigorous modernism with luxurious materials, Rudolph with theatrical gestures like Plexiglas floors, mirrored surfaces, and quirky collections.

Georgis also looks to Japanese architecture and decorative arts for models of "superminimal, clean, modern design" and techniques of enhancing the beauty of natural materials through decorative finishes. He often uses traditional Japanese lacquer as well as French techniques to turn wood cabinetry and architectural paneling and moldings into decorative components of interior ensembles. A door hiding a powder room in a Park Avenue apartment's art-lined entry hall becomes a work of art in itself with wire-brushed ash wood lacquered and gilded in the Japanese *nurimono* tradition. In the same apartment, notes Georgis, the woodwork "has been bleached, it's been wire-brushed to open the pores, and then it's been stained and then waxed. So it's had its hair done," he says, "within an inch of its life. The wood is pushed to the limit." Similarly, kitchen cabinets in Georgis's La Jolla, California, home are made of oak that has been sandblasted, bleached, stained, and then lacquered and hand-rubbed. "It looks natural," says Georgis, "but it's the most unnatural finish on the planet." Another favorite technique, cerusing, derived from a traditional French practice, entails rubbing a contrasting pigment into the wood grain to enhance its effect. Georgis uses cerusing to enrich woodwork in a variety of ways; in his La Jolla library, for instance, the paneling was stained olive brown and cerused to enhance the wild grain of the ash.

Common themes of the decorative arts that interest Georgis include "luxury, craft, design in the service of status and power." This has much to do with the nature of many of his clients, who, according to Georgis, "aspire to similar goals." His client list includes leaders in finance and real estate; he describes them as self-made risk-takers who aim to make their mark with the design of their residences and offices. Developing close relationships, both professional and personal, with his clients, Georgis considers many of them patrons due to their multiple commissions and to their support of his *Gesamtkunstwerk* approach and the extraordinary level of craft needed to achieve it.

Georgis's inclusive and integrated aesthetic is perhaps best summarized in his own home in La Jolla, a 2011 rethinking of a midcentury modern house. Nicknamed "the Akropolis" in reference to his Greek heritage and its hillside setting, the project combines into an architectural autobiography the many

Kyoto, Japan: Temple and gardens

Chinatown Brasserie, New York, 2006: View toward entrance with ceramic sutra holder by Peter Lane and silk lantern by Georgis

Apartment, New York, 2007: Dining room with bronze-framed lacquered-wood paneling depicting idealized Chinese landscapes

themes that characterize his work. For the decorating concept, Georgis cites a narrative of vagabonds: he and Marshall crossed the country like settlers who moved from place to place with Conestoga wagons holding whatever possessions they had accumulated. He also drew on La Jolla's history as an artistic community that is by the beach but has, Georgis notes, "something not-beachy about it." With many residents from the Midwest and the East Coast, La Jolla has "a kind of pretension that I hope this house feels comfortable in. It's not what I would call a beachlike interior."

Respecting the midcentury structure's "Japonesque modern" character, Georgis created a residence whose sources range from gilded Japanese temples (for the tea-paper-clad living room ceiling) to mirrored stair risers that evoke Liberace and Busby Berkeley to a stair railing of hefty nautical rope and wide plank floors with a driftwood finish suitable for a house at the beach to Ultrasuede walls and curtains that evoke "the world of Halston in the 1970s and a hushed luxury." Artwork is integral to the design: a commissioned piece by Kim MacConnel recalls surfboards and tribal art; a landscape design by artist Judy Kameon offers a painterly approach to the mixing of plant materials; contemporary works by Mike Kelley and Ed Ruscha share wall space with paintings of Greek ruins. The distillation of his mature aesthetic, the Akropolis represents Georgis's ambition to create in his own work the quality he witnessed as a child in the buildings of Frank Lloyd Wright: a unique voice.

Park Avenue Apartment

New York, New York
1998, 2004

Postwar, Prewar. *Georgis originally designed this 3,300-square-foot apartment in 1998. It was sold, with some of its furnishings, and redecorated for different clients in 2004. Located in a Gothic Revival building by architect Emery Roth and constructed in 1915, the apartment features a reconfigured plan organized around a rectangular entrance gallery. This area is flanked on one side by a living-dining room and a study (with commanding views south down Park Avenue) and on the other by the kitchen and the bedroom wing. In addition to featuring unusual decorative finishes, such as ash wood treated with an ancient Japanese gilded-grain technique, and exotic materials like backlit onyx, the apartment is furnished with works by Georgis, artists such as Michele Oka Doner, and masters of mid-twentieth-century modernism including Jean Royère, Jacques Adnet, Felix Agostini, and Edward Wormley. The contemporary art collection contains works by Jean-Michel Basquiat, Louise Bourgeois, Ed Ruscha, and David Salle.*

Park Avenue Apartment

Grand New York prewar apartments were planned with discrete entertaining spaces that were to be serviced by large staffs. Things have changed since then, and many of the people who buy these apartments today—often culturally adventurous collectors of contemporary art, such as my clients—live more casually, preferring open spaces and day help. Maids' bedrooms and staff dining rooms are repurposed as eat-in kitchens, family rooms, and playrooms.

In the late 1990s, when I designed this project, the impulse was to make such apartments look like modernist, open-plan spaces, which, in fact, they were not. I guess it was a perverse instinct—something to do with the culture of the time and what was expected of contemporary art collectors. So in this project, originally a traditionally laid-out four-bedroom apartment with an entrance vestibule, living room, and dining room, we tore out all the walls and reconfigured the plan to make it a more open, three-bedroom apartment. The enlarged entrance gallery, created by combining several smaller spaces, flows into the living area, which opens to the dining area, and so on.

The spacious entrance gallery gives way to the living-dining room. Bryan Hunt's bronze sculpture *Daphne* (1979) and Joan Mitchell's *Cypresses* (1975) bring the space to life. An abstract plane of wire-brushed ash wood, lacquered and then gilded in the Japanese *nurimono* tradition, masks the entrance to a powder room. The powder room itself is like being inside a chunk of stone: the wainscot, floor, and lavatory are all fossil stone, and the walls are paneled from waist up in nickel-framed, mercury-gilded antique mirror.

The living and dining areas occupy a single space separated by an internally lit caramel-colored onyx wall. My goal for these spaces was to create a modernist pavilion distinct from the rest of the apartment. This is reinforced by the floor: Combe Brun French limestone paving differentiates it from the wood floors used elsewhere. A draped wall masks an irregularity in the fenestration. The room is furnished with a mixture of twentieth-century and custom-designed fittings, including a suite of upholstered Royère furniture; a sterling-silver-topped coffee table commissioned from artist Michele Oka Doner; and pieces I designed, including a silk-and-wool rug woven by V'Soske and cabinets based on Ming Dynasty models and featuring Japonesque paintings of butterflies and grasses on a gilded background.

In contrast to the more airy, open-plan living-dining pavilion, the library is a hermetic space that can be shut off from the rest of the apartment. It occupies a corner room with views south over Park Avenue made possible by the neighboring low church. The room is paneled in Macassar ebony with antique bronze detail; shuttered pocket doors allow the area to be transformed into a cocoon. A custom mohair sofa, bamboo-inlaid coffee table, and Royère chairs complete the picture of domesticity. Jean-Michel Basquiat's *Self-Portrait with Suzanne* adds a note of irreverence.

The master bedroom is the ultimate refuge from New York and the rest of the apartment. Buttery plaster walls and kidskin-upholstered doors provide a hushed and luxurious backdrop for custom furnishings, including a chaise made from a thick plate of bronze, an Agostini torchère, and a Japanese screen.

Plan, Pre-renovation

Plan, 2004

0 4 8

PAGE 18
Biomorphic French armchair and bronze-and-glass Felix Agostini low table against an illuminated onyx wall in the living room (2004)

OPPOSITE
Living room with Jean Royère Ours Polaire sofa, French lamp, and Georgis-designed cabinet with butterflies and grass (1998)

LEFT
Suite of Jean Royère upholstered
furniture, sterling-silver *Celestial
Pattern* table by Georgis and
Michele Oka Doner, and Andy
Warhol drawing in living room
(2004)

OVERLEAF LEFT
Entrance foyer with Bryan Hunt
bronze sculpture and Joan Mitchell
painting (1998)

OVERLEAF RIGHT
Living room with Royère chairs and
nesting tables, and Gerhard Richter
painting (2004)

Macassar-ebony-paneled library
with custom table and sofa, Erton
chairs, and drawing by Jean-Michel
Basquiat; the window looks south
over Park Avenue (1998)

ABOVE
Kitchen with built-in aquarium, and
Georgis-designed banquette and
Bahia-blue-marble-and-steel table
(1998)

28

I have always been entranced by Mies van der Rohe's use of luxurious materials, such as book-matched, veined marbles and wood veneers. In the stripped-down idiom of modernism, this palette adds warmth and texture. Coaxing the beauty out of materials is important—I've got to make things out of something, so once I've decided on a wood or a stone, it better sing.

LEFT
Onyx, limestone, and mosaic in the master bathroom (2004)

ABOVE
Powder room with mercury-gilded mirror, nickel frames, and fossil stone (1998)

ABOVE
Master bedroom with French desk and chair, Georgis-designed rug, Georges Jouve sconces, and Robert Mapplethorpe photograph (1998)

RIGHT
Master bedroom with cracked-ice carpet, Slug chaise, and bed by Georgis with drawing by Yayoi Kusama (2004)

Modern Icon Restored. *Lever House, built in 1952 as the first all-glass-curtain-wall commercial building in New York City, is an icon of modern architecture and a local and national landmark. Designed by Gordon Bunshaft of Skidmore, Owings & Merrill with interiors by industrial designer Raymond Loewy, the structure comprises a narrow twenty-four-story tower and a raised podium above a large street-level landscaped public plaza designed, but not fully realized, by Isamu Noguchi. The complex was renovated fifty years after its completion by a team consisting of SOM and Georgis, who was responsible for the designs of the exterior and interior public spaces. The lobby accommodates two functions: a reception area for the building's tenants and a gallery for changing exhibitions from the Lever House Art Collection. Georgis restored the original finishes and designed custom furnishings, as well as new elevator cabs. He also oversaw restoration of the exterior landscape in collaboration with landscape architect Ken Smith.*

Lever House

This is a simple project about respect; about sublimating ego, seeing the genius of what is there, honoring it, bringing it back to life. It's about nothing more.

I had worked with the new owner of Lever House, a New York real estate developer and art collector, on a number of residential projects. A modern architecture buff, he bought Lever House in 1998 and later purchased the equally eminent Seagram Building across Park Avenue. What was especially interesting about the project was the owner's vision for Lever House—he wanted to turn it into a sort of corporate club. Because of the limited size of the floor plates, it is especially suitable to a specific type of early-twenty-first-century business— hedge funds and other corporations with financial interests that don't require enormous staffs. The allure of the building is buttressed by the Lever House Art Collection, started by the new owner with the assistance of curator Richard D. Marshall. Site-specific installations, open to the public, are commissioned four times a year from prominent artists.

I was asked to restore the public spaces of both the interior and the exterior. Drawings for the interiors, originally designed by Raymond Loewy, were languishing, uncataloged and inaccessible, at the Library of Congress. All I had to guide our work were vintage photographs. We carefully restored interior finishes, such as stone cladding, a yellow-glass-mosaic accent wall, stainless-steel column covers, and terrazzo floors. New recessed light fixtures were custom-designed to work with existing trims. When it came time to furnish the lobby, it seemed strange to reproduce the Loewy furniture from photographs.

I designed a suite of furniture and a rug that were meant to seem like they belonged there. The chairs are made from sheets of stainless steel folded in the shape of an L (for Lever House); white leather cushions are cantilevered from stainless-steel bases. The table also has a stainless-steel L base; it is topped by a piece of cantilevered glass that takes its cue from the building's cantilevered design.

The one furniture piece that was a departure from Loewy's vision is the reception desk. The building, constructed for a single corporation, was being converted to multitenant use. Modern technology and multiple receptionists had to be accommodated. I'd like to think that the desk is respectful of Bunshaft's building and Loewy's interiors. I used a similar approach for the elevator cabs, since no documentation was available. The walls are clad in floating planes of backlit Corian—a material that did not exist in 1952—and floors are black terrazzo.

Ken Smith, an adventurous and scholarly landscape architect, directed the restoration of the landscape. At the Isamu Noguchi archives, Smith discovered plans by the artist for the Lever House gardens and marble seating, including totemic sculptural elements (never made) in the floating planter that penetrates the wall between the interior lobby and the exterior plaza. Because the New York City Landmarks Commission considered Noguchi's totems fine rather than decorative art, permission to construct them posthumously was denied. But Noguchi had also designed a series of benches for the exterior plaza, and the Landmarks Commission permitted these to be built. Plantings were inspired by period photographs.

Plan

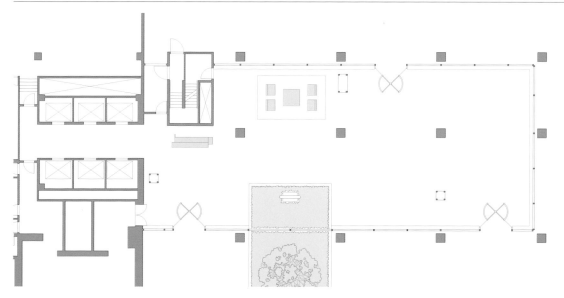

0   6   12

PAGE 33
View of lobby looking toward refurbished yellow-glass-mosaic wall and elevator banks with Georgis-designed walnut, stainless-steel, and powder-coated-aluminum reception desk

OPPOSITE
Lobby with original terrazzo floor, stainless-steel columns, and curtain wall; the interior planter features a marble sculpture by Isamu Noguchi

ABOVE
Exterior view of building with restored curtain wall

Details of the building are reiterated in the interior design. The carpet I designed for the lobby is two shades of green in a grid pattern taken from the exterior curtain wall. It's not meant to be remarkable; it's just meant to seem like it belongs there.

Original stainless-steel-and-glass display cases; Isamu Noguchi bronze sculpture; and Georgis-designed leather-and-stainless-steel chairs, cantilevered-glass-and-stainless-steel table, and wool rug

Georgis-Marshall Townhouse

New York, New York
2001

An Architect's Own. *Georgis and his partner, Richard D. Marshall, live in a renovated five-story, five-thousand-square-foot townhouse on the Upper East Side of Manhattan. Originally constructed around 1910, the building had fallen into disrepair, losing much of its original detailing. Extensive reimagining and reconstruction were required to create a single-family residence and offices for William T. Georgis Architect. The renovation included new exterior facades, front and back landscapes, interior architecture and decoration, and extension into the garden. Georgis's offices are on the lower two floors; the residence occupies the three floors above. The reconfigured townhouse has a complex spatial organization, with a double-height living room at the rear overlooked by a mezzanine library, translucent walls that dissolve interior boundaries, and hanging garden terraces at three levels. The interior is furnished with an eclectic mix of eighteenth-, nineteenth-, and twentieth-century furniture. The art collection includes work by Julian Schnabel, Alex Katz, Jean-Michel Basquiat, Ed Ruscha, and Bruce Nauman.*

Context is important in the design of this house. We live on a wide cross street on the Upper East Side surrounded by predominantly nineteenth- and twentieth-century masonry buildings, just outside the Upper East Side Historic District. I wanted to challenge this traditional context, so I created a smoked-glass modern house.

The open-plan design alleviates the constraints of the not-quite-eighteen-foot building width with a system of doors that creates privacy where appropriate. Views are open from the front to the back of the building—from the street to the rear garden. Curtain walls at the front and back maximize light and create a cat-and-mouse game of exhibitionism and voyeurism with the street. The core of the building, which contains an elevator and mechanical services, is set thirteen feet back from the street; it obscures the view through the house but gives the passersby a teasing peek into the house. A skylight over the stair admits light to the entire building, including an interior guest bathroom with etched-glass walls.

Paul Rudolph's Upper East Side townhouse, later inhabited by Halston, has always been my Rosetta Stone. Both that house and Rudolph's own multistory apartment on Beekman Place are extraordinary; both transgress their sedate neighborhoods. Rudolph's work combines the most refined architectural sensibility with a louche quality. In his own residence, mirrored ceiling beams dematerialize the structure and provide glamour. He installed a Plexiglas bathtub that also serves as a skylight for the room below so that attractive guests could be admired voyeuristically. I wanted to do something similar in spirit in my house—one example is the steam room that stretches across the fifth floor facing the street. It's behind translucent glass, so at night you have to turn certain lights off so your body isn't projected onto the glass like a shadow puppet.

The decoration brings together furnishings old and new, inherited and custom-fabricated. The important thing was to create a vibrant, unorthodox mix that surprises and creates both visual and ideological juxtapositions. In the double-height living room, Julian Schnabel's fifteen-foot-high *Hat Full of Rain* coexists with a gilded Roman Baroque mirror, an antique Roman torso of Herakles, and a mounted moose head. A disco ball from a Veterans of Foreign Wars hall, red velvet sofas, and shearling rug converse provocatively.

In the library, on the mezzanine overlooking the living room, a Billy Haines gray-cashmere-covered sofa and coffee table sit on a hot pink Tibetan wool rug. A salon-style installation of art consists of works by Cindy Sherman, Jean-Michel Basquiat, Ed Ruscha, Michael Hurson, Fred Tomaselli, John Waters, and Raymond Pettibon. The master suite on the top floor, carpeted with leopard-spot broadloom, is furnished with magenta silk curtains salvaged from a relative's Manhattan mansion, a custom-designed stainless-steel bed, artist Scott Burton's steel side tables, and Cornelius Völker's painting *Trash*.

The landscape includes a front garden and a series of three hanging gardens at the rear of the house. The building is severe from the outside, and I wanted plantings that were emotive and doleful, softening the brutality of the city for us and for the pedestrian. A blue Atlas cedar tree underplanted with juniper inhabits a planter at the front of the house. The cedar tree has a weepy Japonesque, almost emotional quality. A large gingko tree on the street is underplanted seasonally; one year it was agave, which is not something generally associated with the Upper East Side. The back garden is paved in enormous granite monoliths and planted with Dutchman's pipe, pachysandra, and bamboo.

Plans

0   4   8

Fourth Floor

Third Floor

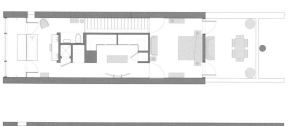

Second Floor

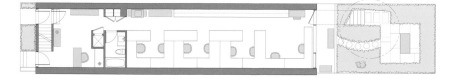

First Floor

PAGE 38
Street facade with glass curtain wall; in the second-floor foyer are an Alex Katz painting and Alexander Calder mobile

OPPOSITE
View from entrance to kitchen, dining, and living room featuring William Dobson Plexiglas table, Corian counter and island, Dorothy Schindele barstools, and Alex Katz painting (reflected in mirrored screen)

ABOVE
Dining room with eighteenth-century parcel-gilt onyx-top table, Bakelite lamp, French nineteenth-century corpus, and drawing by Christopher Wool

RIGHT
Roman torso of Herakles, second century A.D., in dining room

OPPOSITE
Foyer with T. H. Robsjohn-Gibbings table, blue Saint-Gobain glass chairs, Alexander Calder mobile, and Lynda Benglis ceramic sculpture

ABOVE
French armchair of about 1950,
stuffed rabbit, 1977 Plexiglas
side table by Barbara Mortimer,
and contemporary drawings and
photographs in the library

OPPOSITE
Living room with shearling rug,
Georgis-designed zebra-silk-velvet
slipper chairs, Maison Jansen
Coromandel-topped coffee table,
Julian Schnabel painting, vintage
disco ball, and marble fireplace

The interior decoration is about juxtaposition, about dialogue between past and present. I'm interested in different periods of history in the fine and decorative arts. Why not hang Jack Pierson's Lover *over a Fortuny-upholstered Venetian bed from the late nineteenth century?*

ABOVE
Master bathroom with black granite floors, white Corian lavatory, mounted volcanic rock from Santorini, and nineteenth-century Dutch mirror

OPPOSITE
Guest bedroom with nineteenth-century gilt and Fortuny-upholstered Venetian bed and Jack Pierson word sculpture

East Side Townhouse, New York, 2004: Roman mirror in the living room

Sun Kings & Queens

Portrait of Louis XIV, after 1701:
Painting from the workshop of Hyacinthe Rigaud

Architectural historians often focus attention on architects and their work rather than on architects and their clients. But would Fallingwater exist without patron Edgar J. Kaufmann Sr., Versailles without Louis XIV, the Farnsworth House without Dr. Edith Farnsworth? William Georgis openly acknowledges the serendipitous results of the strong relationships between him and his clients. "I try to make a place in the world for them," he says, "to create a physical environment that gives them visibility, to provide a backdrop against which they become the protagonists." The result is often transformational. One of his clients noted, "He really opened our eyes…He gently pushes you against your comfort level, and then you see."

Georgis dubs his clients the "merchant princes of the twenty-first century," a network from the arenas of real estate, finance, publishing, and art who often know each other personally and professionally. He describes them as hard-driving, self-starting, competitive, and culturally adventurous, sharing an appetite for luxury and a desire to live well. Above all, Georgis says, "They want to transcend the ordinary"—to make their own marks with their personal environments. The corollary is that clients don't come to Georgis for safe design. Those who hire him are often willing to take risks with design that a lot of people wouldn't take. "How many clients are going to encourage you to design crime-scene carpets with blood-spattered interiors?" he asks.

Georgis's clients, primarily Manhattan-based, are often attracted to the status of the Upper East Side, but not to the status quo. Therein lies the tension that cues Georgis's designs for them: their personal antipathy to convention is reflected in his strategies, which often transgress conventional boundaries of taste and style. Georgis's clients buy desirable real estate because it is spacious and convenient but challenge its stuffiness and traditional aesthetic by hiring him.

For an early project in a prewar Park Avenue building, for instance, Georgis "blew open the plan" and tore out all the walls of the public rooms, reconfiguring the space into a free-flowing sequence of entry, living, and dining areas separated only by low walls and translucent screens. He designed fresh Moderne details and used luxurious materials to define a new expression within a traditional shell.

Not unlike the geography of Edith Wharton's Gilded Age, which centered on Manhattan yet encompassed places like Newport, the New York of Georgis's clients extends beyond Manhattan's Upper East Side and stylish downtown neighborhoods to include Palm Beach, the Caribbean, the eastern

Two projects for the same patron:
Corridor, East Side Townhouse, New York, 2004

Sitting room, Beach House, Southampton, 2003

end of Long Island, and the far west of Montana and Colorado, where he designs their vacation homes. The nature of Georgis's work also falls within the tradition of Gilded Age architects like Richard Morris Hunt and Stanford White, who created sophisticated, cultured environments that integrated architecture with fine and decorative arts for the merchant princes of the late nineteenth and early twentieth centuries. For Georgis's clients too, their homes become a medium for establishing their position and importance.

Georgis sees his role as understanding what his clients want, even when they do not explicitly articulate their desires. He aims not to have a recognizable "William Georgis look" but to create projects that in their variety reflect the diverse nature of his clients. "It's about making sense of their worlds," he says. "They want to be grounded and they want an appropriate stage set. If that doesn't happen, it doesn't work." One of Georgis's patrons says that she is always surprised when she visits other homes he has designed, observing that each reflects the owners' tastes. She describes his projects as "real collaborations. Bill listens and works with each individual to create something special for them."

Georgis characterizes his relationships with his clients as "a kind of marriage"—a statement reflecting the nature of his highly customized work, which involves many conversations about personal needs and desires, as well as shopping and travel together. For some, Georgis goes beyond the design of their residence to assist with the entire process of buying, designing, furnishing, accessorizing, moving into, and living in their homes. His work may start with the search for the right apartment and continue to the design of the owner's lifestyle—helping to purchase china, silverware, linens, even suggesting a florist and framing family photographs. And in a city where "part of making one's mark is to inhabit a world that involves art," Georgis's partner, curator Richard D. Marshall, is a valuable collaborator.

While many of Georgis's clients are "super-successful," some live modestly until they hire him to design their first significant home. When they move into their new residences, they bring their art and leave their furniture. Georgis typically designs or selects all furnishings; he also may help to hire staff, prepare service manuals for the household, or provide photos of tabletops as models to follow. One patron, for whom Georgis has done multiple projects, says he and his wife moved from a two-bedroom apartment with sweaters and unwanted Christmas presents in the oven and a Ralph Lauren sofa into a six-thousand-square-foot Park Avenue apartment. Until he met Georgis, "We had no idea what the possibilities were." His wife adds, "He would educate us, explaining the history of the furniture maker and why people think a particular piece is good, giving us books and showing us photographs of where the pieces were originally installed." Her husband recalls Georgis recommending the purchase of a suite of Jean Royère furniture for a sum he never would have

Two projects for the same patron: Living room, Palm Beach Apartment, 2006; outdoor seating area, Park Avenue Penthouse, New York, 2003

Two projects for the same patron: Dining area, Soho Apartment, New York, 2008; dining area, Montana Residence, Big Sky, 2010

imagined spending—a suite that then had to be reupholstered. "But we learned," he says. "The result was great: Bill is good with beauty." Georgis says that they now tell him that he "spoiled them because they have become educated about quality and about comfort. But they are happy about that."

Georgis considers some clients, with whom he has had long-term relationships, to be patrons. According to one, who suggests he was elevated to patron status after two commissions, he returns to Georgis for many of his residential and commercial projects because "Bill understands what I want. He is very good at taking a strong hand with a client, especially a sophisticated client." He adds, "He respects what I want; I respect what he delivers." Many of Georgis's patrons have recommended him to their friends, establishing a close coterie of clients who work and socialize in the same orbit. Within that group there is a high level of trust between architect and patrons: they let his ideas push them past their limits. One client describes the evolution of her relationship with Georgis over the course of her apartment renovation. "When he first showed me a sample of mica for the walls of the new foyer, I said, 'No way!'" Now, she says, "Anything he says is perfect and right, and I'm sorry I didn't do every single thing that he originally proposed."

D.A. and N.S.

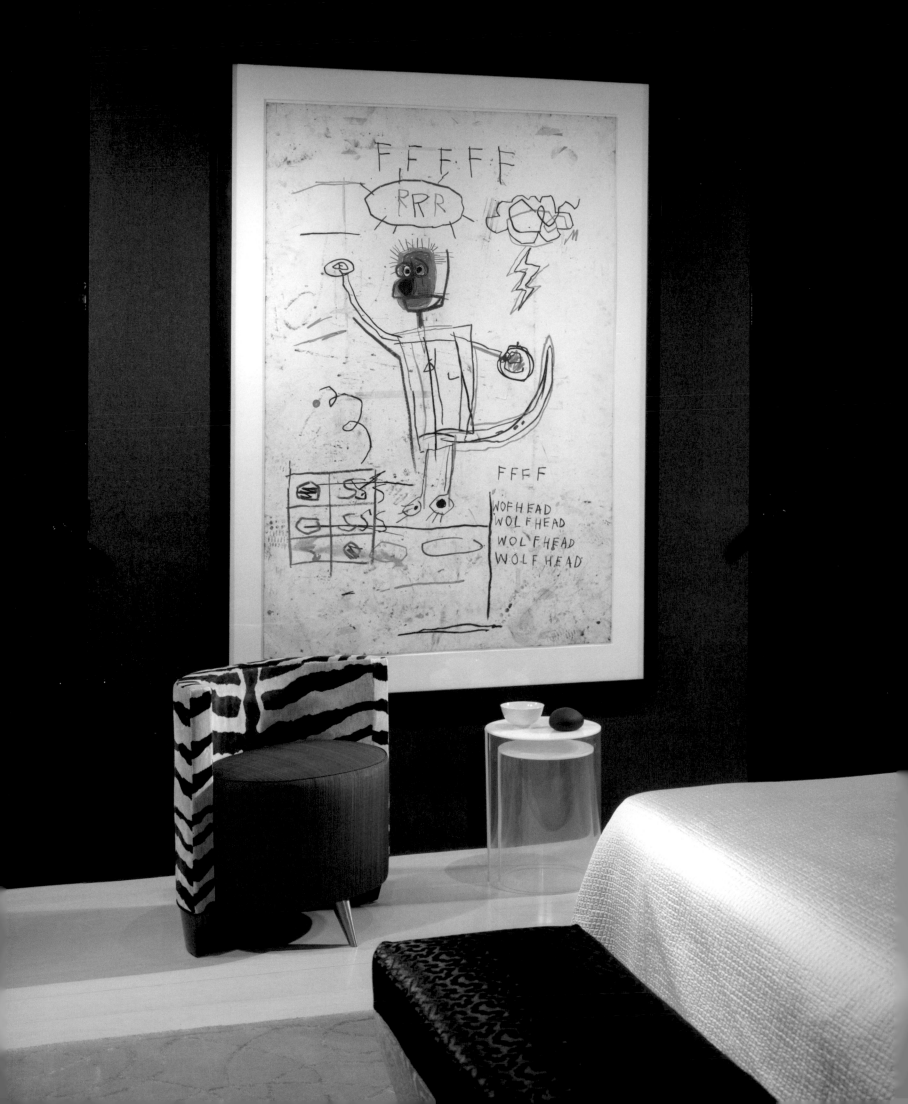

Apartment at the Carlyle Hotel

New York, New York
2001

Room at the Top. *Georgis designed this apartment, originally configured as a two-bedroom hotel suite, to take advantage of spectacular views in three directions. All the interior partitions were removed to create a 1,240-square-foot, open-plan, one-bedroom residence. The apartment is organized around a walnut-paneled wall that bisects the space; the living room and library are situated at opposite ends, with the master suite hidden behind. The apartment provides a setting for the couple's art collection, with works by Juan Gris, Joan Miró, Alexander Archipenko, Joaquín Torres-García, Jean-Michel Basquiat, and Louise Bourgeois. The furnishings, including custom-designed and important twentieth-century pieces, coexist with the modernity of the art collection.*

Apartment at the Carlyle Hotel

New York's Carlyle Hotel is legendary—a place of great glamour designed in the late 1920s with neo-Baroque interiors by Dorothy Draper. While most of the Art Deco tower houses hotel suites, a precious few apartments are privately owned. Apartment owners enjoy all hotel amenities, including maid service, concierge service, and room service, making city life idyllic *and* sybaritic. This is the second apartment I've designed at the Carlyle for these South American clients. When an apartment on a very high floor became available, they nabbed it and called me.

The idea was simple: to convert a two-bedroom apartment into an open-plan one-bedroom aerie. I wanted my clients to be able to escape the madness of the city and be coddled by hotel services while enjoying breathtaking views over Central Park, the George Washington Bridge, the New Jersey Palisades, and midtown Manhattan. I conceived the minimal design to focus attention on the views and the fine things in the apartment. The rich but subdued palette of materials includes white ash, French walnut, bronze, stainless steel, French limestone, Belgian black marble, and cashmere. The apartment was intended to be a place from which to contemplate the city—to catch a breath before reengaging.

This simple mission was not easy to accomplish. Opening the plan was difficult because of existing columns, pipes, and risers. Since the Carlyle is in a landmark district, we couldn't replace the windows without returning to the 1929 configuration. This would have eliminated the large picture windows that were inserted after the building was completed. Another challenge was the apartment's low ceilings.

To open the space as much as possible, I developed a scheme that removed all interior room dividers and finishes. An especially thick French-walnut-clad wall organizes the plan while concealing structural columns and accommodating library shelving. The living room and library are at opposite ends of the wall. Floors were paved with wide planks of bleached ash, and walls were kept strictly white: the whole was to be luminous and ethereal.

Under the picture window in the living room, a large Turkish-inspired daybed upholstered in suede and flanked by leather-clad light-box side tables provides a comfortable perch from which to contemplate the views. I designed a rug in pale blue silk and wool to bring the sky into the apartment. A wide white stripe at one end of the rug registers the gallery that connects the living room and library. Alexander Archipenko's *Female Torso* poses on a floating stainless-steel console.

The living room is sparely furnished with a pair of French armchairs from the 1950s, a Jean-Michel Frank guéridon table, a pair of Pierre Chareau side tables, a Serge Mouille floor lamp, and a small dining table I designed with a bronze base and shagreen top. The design and furnishings were kept simple and minimal to provide visual space for paintings by Juan Gris, Giorgio Morandi, and Joaquín Torres-García and a pair of Louise Bourgeois bronze sculptures. A small kitchen off the living room functions as a butler's pantry; most meals are either taken at restaurants or provided by room service.

The library, situated at the other end of the walnut wall, is furnished simply, with a desk, pull-up chair, and pair of Josef Hoffmann barrel-backed chairs. Keith Haring drawings and a painting by Robert Harms breathe life and color into the room.

A concealed door in the walnut wall leads to the bedroom—a very different experience. While the rest of the apartment is light and white, the bedroom is upholstered in charcoal cashmere. The dark walls focus attention on the spectacular views west over Central Park and south along Madison Avenue and create a lair perfect for hibernation. The severity of the design is relieved by punches of color from Jean-Michel Basquiat's oil stick drawing and a custom-designed orange and zebra-patterned silk-velvet vanity chair with a stiletto leg. The chair is a reference to the wife's great sense of fashion.

The public spaces of the Carlyle were designed in the 1920s in a voluptuously decorative style that has since been updated. In contrast, this super-minimalist apartment, admittedly one with a rich palette, is a little startling. There's something transgressive about it, which I love.

Plan

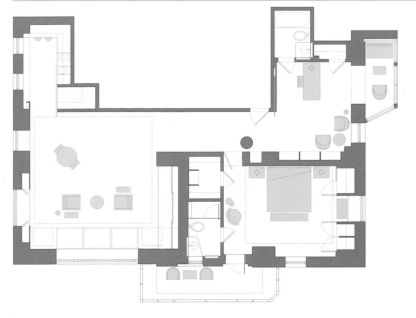

0   4   8

PAGE 54
Master bedroom featuring Georgis's Stiletto stool in zebra silk velvet, orange silk satin, and nickel; on the wall is a Jean-Michel Basquiat drawing

OPPOSITE
View from living room toward library with walnut wall, stainless-steel-encased column, bleached floor, and painting by Joaquín Torres-García; on the silk-and-wool carpet in the foreground are bronze sculptures by Louise Bourgeois

View over Madison Avenue from terrace

When I found the Josef Hoffmann chairs and table, the original upholstery and velvet tabletop were very worn. I left them in this original condition, time-weathered museum pieces in an otherwise pristine, modern space.

LEFT
Bookcases in walnut wall and Keith Haring and Joel Shapiro drawings in the library

ABOVE
Library with Josef Hoffmann chairs and table with Eugene Printz torchère and painting by Robert Harms

ABOVE
Gray-cashmere-upholstered walls
and Georgis-designed parchment
bedside tables, bed, horsehair-
covered bench, and rug in the
master bedroom

OPPOSITE
Living room with floating stainless-
steel commode, low leather-clad
and suede-upholstered banquette,
Alexander Archipenko torso, and
Juan Gris painting

in the same building (see page 48) was limited by the existing structure and perimeter walls; this penthouse offered greater architectural opportunity. The objective was to create a guest suite on the rooftop of the building, replacing an existing aluminum-sided staff apartment with a 980-square-foot, one-bedroom modern pavilion with walls of floor-to-ceiling glass. The pavilion is surrounded on three sides by terraces created in collaboration with landscape architect Edmund D. Hollander. The organizing element of the interior is a deep wall housing a bar, television, and desk that can be fully concealed by stainless-steel pocket doors; the wall separates the living room from the bedroom, bathroom, and kitchen. Furnishings include vintage pieces by such designers as Jean Royère and Milo Baughman, as well as custom-designed pieces by Georgis for both the interior (such as a shearling banquette) and the exterior (stainless-steel dining furniture, rocking chairs, and a settee). The project features works by Donald Judd and John Morris.

Make It Fabulous

This project has a wildly extravagant program—a guest suite–cum–summer house on the rooftop of a prewar Park Avenue apartment building. The garden folly is perhaps reminiscent of Marie Antoinette's *petit hameau*. The clients could send guests from their main apartment to private quarters four floors above. The wife said, "Our guests won't be right on top of us because they'll be way up on top of us!" In addition, al fresco cocktails and dinners could be hosted in the private garden. I wanted to create a building in the nature of Philip Johnson's Glass House, Mies van der Rohe's Farnsworth House, or even Mies's Barcelona pavilion—open-plan structures that seamlessly meld interior and exterior space.

One goal was to create an idyllic pavilion or folly in an Elysian garden—to devise a space where you could leave the city behind. The garden is partially surrounded by high parapet walls and acid-etched glass walls that allow light in as they block city views. A dry bed of pebbles in the Japanese style suggests a stream of water with a border of luxuriant foxtail grasses. A weeping hemlock holds center stage, and towering bamboo planted in strategic spots holds the city at bay. Expansive areas, replete with my custom furnishings, are set aside for dining, sunning, and conversing. The odd water tower visible in the distance does nothing to disrupt the calm serenity.

The new pavilion, while limited by the footprint of the original construction on the roof, takes advantage of the gardens. The vocabulary is more hard-edged than that of the main apartment below. The structure features a glass curtain wall with large sliding glass doors; it is appointed with stainless-steel and Corian cabinetry and a slate fireplace. Indoor and outdoor paving is Valders limestone.

I kept the interior palette cool, with small bursts of color—for example, the violet-blue lava-stone top of the coffee table I designed for the living room. A spectacular untitled stack piece by Donald Judd, with planes of translucent green Plexiglas, brings the garden indoors, while Royère's Small Oeuf and Sculpture chairs, upholstered in velvet and silk, introduce a quality of voluptuousness. I designed a silk rug and a shearling-upholstered banquette for the living room. The bedroom is lined with American black walnut wainscoting that projects at one point to form a desk. Japanese ceramics commingle with John Morris drawings, a handwoven rug, and a riotous pink-and-green silk bed coverlet.

Plan

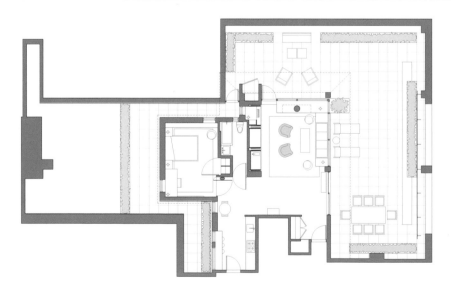

0 4 8

PAGE 64
Pavilion in stainless steel, glass, and slate with Valders limestone paving indoors and out

ABOVE
Outdoor seating area with Georgis-designed stainless-steel Chris rockers and cast-glass tables

I have always been fascinated by the glass architecture of modern architects like Mies van der Rohe and Philip Johnson, which seamlessly integrates exterior and interior spaces. This project presented the opportunity to design a glass pavilion, but in an unexpected setting: on the rooftop of a prewar masonry apartment building in New York City.

ABOVE
Donald Judd galvanized-steel-and-
Plexiglas sculpture in living room

RIGHT
Living room with stainless-steel wall
housing bar and desk

LEFT
Bedroom with John Morris
drawings and walnut wainscoting;
the wainscoting projects in a bed
and desk

ABOVE
Milo Baughman swivel chair,
Japanese candlestand, and vase in
the bedroom

Beach House
Southampton, New York
2003, 2012

Colonial Revival Revived. *This ten-thousand-square-foot, seven-bedroom Colonial Revival house, located on an oceanfront site in Southampton, was originally an accessory building on a large estate. It has been renovated and expanded numerous times over its history, most recently by Georgis, who designed two new wings and decorated the interior as a summer home for a Manhattan-based family. The plan of the house had evolved into a rambling, mazelike series of rooms; Georgis clarified the layout by creating large open spaces out of small clusters of rooms and by making strategic architectural interventions. These included an entry gallery and stair leading to the former ballroom, now a living room with ocean views. While the exteriors of Georgis's additions respect the formal historical style of the original structure, the interiors feature custom-designed furniture and vintage pieces from Europe, Asia, and Africa as well as the clients' extensive collection of contemporary photographs by Nan Goldin, Wolfgang Tillmans, Lynn Davis, and others. The landscape was designed by Mario Nievera.*

When my clients, for whom I've completed multiple residential and commercial works, telephoned me about this project, they were concerned that the house and its furnishings (dark finishes, antiques, and chintz) spoke more to the Southampton of the nineteenth century than to that of the twenty-first. But I was confident we could create the cool, casual, breezy summer escape they dreamed of. The house has over the years donned a mantle of grandeur commensurate with its neighbors. The grandeur would have to be transformed for these particular clients.

We converted a formal dining room on axis with the entry into a more casual area for family meals and relaxation off the swimming pool. The adjacent living room became a family room, while a new living room was created in the former ballroom on the second floor. As the dunes had gradually grown higher, ocean views from the first floor had been blocked. Past owners had jacked the house up and built an elaborate upper-level ballroom furnished in Belle Epoque splendor. I replaced the concealed stair leading to the ballroom with a more public grand stair. Since the original renovation, I have added two symmetrical wings, one for staff quarters and a spacious guest suite, the other for the children.

Once the architectural problems were solved, we were able to focus on the decor. The clients did not want the historical style of the exterior to constrain the interior. The husband is a modernist at heart, a collector of contemporary art, and so the mandate was to "clean house"—to make a place where he and his family could relax and entertain all summer long. The sophisticated yet informal environment would also integrate their art collection and accommodate the family's entertainment and recreation schedule.

My strategy was to decorate against the architecture, but in a respectful way. I transformed the character of the house with interiors done entirely in white: whitewashed oak floors, white walls, white rugs, and white upholstery. The white finishes unify the interiors and give them a clean look and a kind of lightness that suits the seaside location.

Antique and new furnishings are juxtaposed throughout the house. The dining room–cum–sitting room is furnished with a walnut table, simple dining chairs, a plaster chandelier, nineteenth-century Korean ceramic lamps, 1950s French-oak-and-rattan chairs, and an Yves Klein coffee table. In other rooms, furniture and objects from Europe, Africa, and Asia mix with midcentury modern and custom pieces. The overall effect is distinctly non-chintzy—there is an unexpected vibrance and glamour hidden behind the traditional exterior.

The new second-story living room is the premier indoor entertaining space. My clients and I eschewed formal seating arrangements for casual seating and billiards. I designed a burl-wood coffee table and surrounded it with overscaled cotton-covered slipper chairs. The modernist pool table covered in turquoise baize anchors the other end of the room, and 1940s French lanterns hang at different heights to evoke a Japanese festival.

The interior also offers a clean, neutral setting for the client's art collection. Art adviser Richard D. Marshall assembled a collection of contemporary photography by such artists as Nan Goldin, Vanessa Beecroft, and Spencer Tunick that focuses on images of nature and the human body—themes particularly relevant to a place intended for leisurely summer pursuits.

Plan, First Floor

Plan, Second Floor

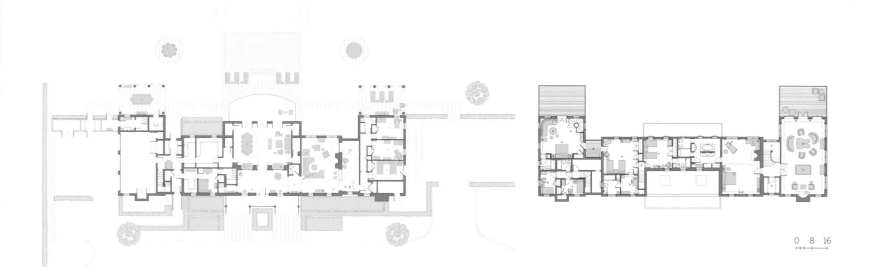

0   8   16

PAGE 73
Oceanside facade

OPPOSITE
Living room with 1940s French glass lanterns, Georgis-designed slipper chairs, and burl-wood coffee table

ABOVE
Walnut refectory table, plaster chandelier, and Walter Niedermayr photographs in the dining room

OPPOSITE
Living room with Roche-Bobois stainless-steel-and-leather chairs and photograph by Sam Samore

ABOVE
Entry gallery with pickled-oak floors, African chair, Gary Hume sculpture, and Nan Goldin photograph

RIGHT
Family room with low banquette, J. Mendel mink pillow, nineteenth-century marble reproduction of one of Selene's horses from the Parthenon, and Spencer Tunick photograph

Reading Between the Lines

As a child, William Georgis developed a passion not only for the bricks and mortar of architecture but also for its representation in movies, magazines, and miniatures. He viewed photographs as entrées to other worlds and his beloved Thorne Miniature Rooms at the Art Institute of Chicago as "models for stage sets." These representations, Georgis came to realize, were as much about the stories told by the rooms as about the rooms themselves. Today he cites as inspirations the movie *Sabrina,* with its evocation of Long Island's Gold Coast; the cinematic Art Moderne style concocted by the head of MGM's art department, Cedric Gibbons; and the glamorously shadowed film noir of movies like Orson Welles's *The Lady from Shanghai.* Georgis is intrigued with the capacity of movie sets—put together "with hair spray and cotton candy"—to convey the essence of an idea. Images like these have informed his aesthetic and are important project references.

Like any good storyteller, Georgis tries to carry the viewer along in time and space, crafting not only the big picture but also the compelling and memorable detail. His design for a powder room, for instance, tells the story of an over-the-hill starlet in a

The Lady from Shanghai, *1947: Rita Hayworth in the climactic scene of Orson Welles's film*

Chinatown Brasserie, New York, 2006: Silk damask lantern

film noir, who, enraged at her ravaged face, shoots up the mirrors. Preeminent among the architect's storytelling interiors is his design for Chinatown Brasserie, inspired by Josef von Sternberg's movie *Shanghai Gesture,* in which a Hollywood version of a vast Shanghai nightclub of the 1940s has a central role. For this project Georgis wanted to create a place where "a scorned woman with bee-stung lips could slap a cad in any corner." Diners experience the space cinematically: the open plan, which uses level changes and decorative screens to define several dining and bar areas, offers oblique views into opium-bed-like booths and a slice of a Chinese-moon-gated garden. And just as today movies like *Shanghai Gesture* might be appreciated for their campiness, Georgis's restaurant has a self-consciously ironic camp quality in its juxtaposition of overscaled Chinese lanterns with commissioned works by well-known artists like Robert Kushner and Peter Lane and hand-painted wallpapers by Gracie.

While Chinatown Brasserie was a highly scenographic setting created for the general public, most of Georgis's narratives are developed for private residences and therefore are less explicit, though still with an element of theatricality. Interiors are often developed as an enfilade—a sequence of rooms, in which each space is discrete and has its own decorative theme yet is visually and spatially linked to the next. Every room expresses its own distinctive role via its decorative theme;

Montana Residence, Big Sky, 2010: Bar decorated with Art Deco mirror, zebra upholstery, leather trim, and tusks

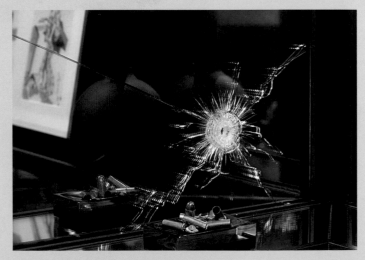

Georgis-Marshall Residence, La Jolla, 2011: Bullet hole and casings in the powder room

Palm Beach Apartment, Florida, 2006: Martinique banana-leaf wallpaper, Chinoiserie commode, and Monchhichi stuffed monkeys in the cabana

American Hospital of Paris 2003 International Designer Showhouse, New York: Bedroom for an imaginary deranged woman with red satin sheets, black rubber coverlet, lipstick-stained cigarette butts, and a phone off the hook

people progress through the spaces like chapters in a novel or scenes in a film.

Georgis's narratives derive from his reading of the clients and their personal stories. "They expect a larger-than-life backdrop—they want drama that's spectacular," Georgis says. This strategy proves especially successful in the vacation houses he has designed. In an apartment in Palm Beach, for example, itself a kind of stage set created by architects like Addison Mizner in the early twentieth century, Georgis's Technicolor palette and monkey imagery spoof and pay homage to the resort setting. Here, like so much of Palm Beach, the new world has outdone the old in style and charm. For another client's log house in Montana, Georgis created a riff on the Wild West, complete with a veneer of hand-notched logs decorating the great room, a stuffed bobcat in the rafters, a custom moose-antler sofa, and birch-bark furnishings upholstered in cashmere.

The Montana project also represents one of Georgis's favorite narratives, the story of settlers crossing the country with possessions gathered from many cultures. "I'm always intrigued by this idea of vagabonds," Georgis notes, "and how transient we are. People are always moving places and taking their things with them. I ask how I can tell that story through design." A master at deploying decorative elements as props, Georgis creates tableaux where objects are in dialogue across time and space. These mise-en-scènes often tell personal stories as well: one corner of the great room in Montana comprises

Upper East Side Townhouse, New York, 2011 (project): Rendering showing dining rotunda with rusticated glass-block walls and a floor of glass blocks set in white marble; images from storyboard presentation of design concepts include the Pantheon in Rome, igloo, photograph of an iceberg by Lynn Davis, Jacques Charpentier dining chairs, puzzle table by the Simmonets, and Louis XV rock crystal chandelier

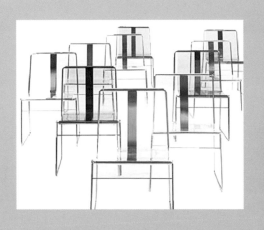

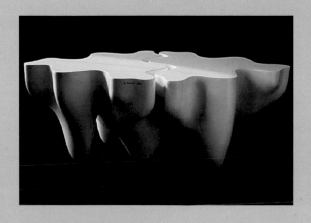

Upper East Side Townhouse, New York, 2011 (project): Rendering showing library with fur-draped walls, horn furnishings, and a bearskin rug;
images from storyboard presentation of design concepts include Lina Loos's fur bedroom designed by Adolf Loos, Alexander McQueen dress, outfit
by Alexander McQueen, Josephine's bedroom in the château de Malmaison, horn chair, and desk by Emile-Jacques Ruhlmann

a limousine-scaled custom daybed upholstered in Scottish cashmere with birch-bark arms and legs wrapped in kidskin and ornamented with overscaled nailheads, a side table supported on tusks, a French ceramic lamp by Mark Etlin, Italian sconces, and artwork by Susan Collis against a spectacular backdrop of the Rocky Mountains. The ensemble conjures an image of exotic rusticity that is cued by the Montana setting and tells a story about the owner's journey to get there.

The vagabond narrative also informed Georgis's renovation of a townhouse on Manhattan's Upper East Side. As he recounts, "The client said, 'Well, I don't really know why I bought this twenty-five-million-dollar house.' I said, 'Because it's beautiful and it's well located.' The client responded, 'Yes, but I don't really belong here.' I said, 'That's what the design is going to be about.'" Georgis then developed a decorative scheme for the house on the theme of provisional habitation, compiling precedent images that ranged from igloos to Napoleon's luxurious tents and furnishings used in his battle campaigns. To show his ideas to the client, Georgis created a series of evocative renderings and an impressionistic storyboard like the ones used by moviemakers. Not the typical client presentation, the nineteen-page storyboard took the client on a scenographic tour of his house, combining long shots of the Pantheon in Rome and close-ups of fishing holes cut in ice with black-fur-draped rooms and black-leather-grommeted fashions by Alexander McQueen.

2009 Kips Bay Show House, New York:
Survival gear in a "panic room"

2009 Kips Bay Show House, New York: "Panic room"
with Russ Meyer's Faster, Pussycat! Kill! Kill!
on the screen and an oxygen tank

While most of Georgis's interiors are created for real clients, he has also constructed narratives for imaginary ones, most notably in two New York decorator show houses. For the American Hospital of Paris 2003 International Designer Showhouse and the 2009 Kips Bay Show House, Georgis created highly stylized settings—a bedroom for a woman akin to the deranged character played by Glenn Close in the film *Fatal Attraction* and a "panic room" where people could "hunker down in style" (to wait out the financial meltdown). These rooms are not so much showcases of interior design trends—as is typical for rooms in these venues—as film sets or backdrops for dramatic action replete with props such as lipstick-stained cigarette butts and oxygen masks and videos providing additional narrative motifs. These interiors share with Georgis's projects for real clients the theme of storytelling through design and decoration.

D.A. and N.S.

Gilded Age Regilded. *For this residence on Manhattan's Upper East Side, Georgis renovated the interior of a historic limestone mansion to create a seven-story, twelve-thousand-square-foot home for a real estate executive and his family. The first and second floors include a smoking room, dining room, breakfast room, butler's pantry, living room, and library. The upper floors contain the family's private quarters, with a media room and outdoor terrace on the top floor. The basement holds the kitchen, service areas, and a gym. Historic details on the first two floors were retained and, where necessary, re-created; the upper floors required a gut renovation. Georgis kept the original circulation: a grand stairway that connects the first and second floors and an enclosed, private stairway that serves the family quarters. The interior decor mixes custom-designed furnishings with historic and contemporary pieces. The clients are avid collectors of contemporary art, and the house presents the works of more than thirty artists, from Pablo Picasso to Andy Warhol and Cy Twombly.*

I had worked on numerous projects for these clients when they asked me to help with this new residence. The husband describes himself as a junkie—an art junkie. Although typically drawn to modern design and contemporary art, he was intrigued by this Beaux-Arts mansion, a former consular residence (and home of Pia Zadora), and we both saw the potential for a provocative dialogue between past and present. Our strategy was to reinforce the architectural context and at the same time to decorate against it. Elaborate traditional plaster wall paneling was restored, for instance, to showcase cutting-edge contemporary art.

The first two floors retained much of their intricate detail; the clients and I decided to respect and maintain, even re-create, this detail wherever possible. We made molds of what was left of the original elements and fabricated new castings to fill missing parts. The upper levels of the house, previously a maze of offices, meeting rooms, and bedrooms, were instead reconfigured and designed in a modern vocabulary. Throughout we wanted to maintain a mix of furnishings from over four centuries.

Each room of the townhouse was to have a distinct aesthetic, which I developed with an eye toward the clients' collections and a desire to create unique spaces. The husband has a restless eye and an insatiable appetite for novelty, with an appreciation of such random objects as prehistoric skeletons and bullfighting uniforms. The art was the wild card: I never knew what would go where, since the collection constantly changes.

The ground-level foyer, missing its original floor, was repaved in an abstracted version of a traditional inlaid-stone checkerboard. Facing the street is the smoking room, where I wanted to create a masculine refuge—a dark sexy room where Tom Wesselmann's luscious-lipped

Smoker #6 and John Chamberlain's small tangle of colorful metals announce male interests. Walls upholstered in dark gray Ultrasuede, a custom-designed rug based on chance and pick-up sticks, and slipper lounges covered in gray shearling create the desired ambience. Stalactites, cloisonné-topped tables, Italian glass, and seventeenth-century pewter candlesticks add exotic elements.

The dining room and adjacent breakfast room, luminous spaces also situated on the ground floor, are immediately adjacent to a lush garden. I wanted the dining room to work for small and large dinner parties and to provide a contrast to the garden and breakfast room as well. The dining room contains a round rosewood table, custom-designed with concentric extensions, and Marc Newson's Komed chairs under a Louis XV chandelier. An ethereal late de Kooning, bold Serra oil stick drawing, and green Warhol self-portrait somehow work with a pair of eighteenth-century French tulipwood and Coromandel-lacquered commodes.

The breakfast room very deliberately relates to the garden with its colorful floral rug and bright orange silk curtains. The clients' Rorschach painting by Warhol prompted me to drip ink on a paper lantern. White-vinyl-upholstered Italian chairs freshen the palette around the sculptural bronze 1970s table by French designer Fred Brouard.

Living rooms, the most public rooms of a house, are expected to reflect the character of the owner. This room had beautiful original architectural detail and a magnificent mantle, which was restored. But for these clients, we wanted the decoration to challenge the status quo and defy expectation. The clients rejected conventional furniture plans, instead pushing for "something different." We dismissed the usual rule of thumb for a living room—to create at least two seating groups. Rather, a single round sofa resting on steel fin legs and upholstered in elephant-hide-colored velvet accompanies a limestone-topped coffee

Plans, First, Second, and Third Floors

Plans, Fourth, Fifth, and Sixth Floors

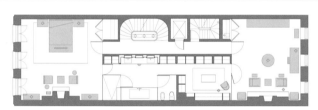

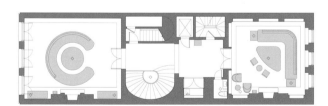

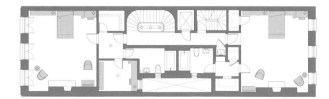

0 4 8

PAGE 92
Ultrasuede-upholstered smoking room with Tom Wesselmann painting over an Art Nouveau mantle, Georgis's shearling slipper chair, and John Chamberlain sculpture

OPPOSITE
Stair hall with refurbished moldings and railing, Cold Spring granite paving, aubergine wool-and-silk stair runner, and stack of Andy Warhol boxes

table on a base resembling an engagement ring. I designed the silk-and-wool rug by standing on a ladder and dripping ink onto Japanese paper. More historic furnishings mediate the modernity of the sofa, coffee table, and rug, while the extraordinary Cy Twombly and Franz Kline paintings and Jeff Koons hanging *Dog Pool with Panty* take the room in a different direction altogether.

The library on the second floor was a fascinating decorating opportunity. Within the context of the original millwork, I developed a phantasmagorical cabinet of curiosities. Ebonized millwork delimits the space, while the mirrored ceiling dissolves any sense of scale—you lose yourself here. I designed stainless-steel chainmail curtains, a black rabbit rug, an L-shaped Chesterfield leather sofa with skunk pillows, and a coffee table made out of shells. Furnishings also include Bugatti chairs, a table made of horn, and side tables consisting of large blocks of anthracite that seem fit for a natural history museum. A large and dramatic 1960s chrome ribbon chandelier, reflected in the mirrored ceiling, completes the furnishings. The curiosities within this setting include various natural-history specimens as well as a wonderfully apt Damien Hirst medicine cabinet.

In the urban bedrooms I design, I try to provide refuge from the chaos of the city with pale palettes, sumptuous textures, and atmospheric lighting. The master bedroom follows that strategy—to a point. China white walls, Combe Brun limestone wainscoting, and a custom-designed geometric rug in eucalyptus and ochre tones work to create a calming backdrop—but a calming backdrop that begs to be challenged. The bed is fabricated from quarter-inch-thick plates of polished stainless steel and is topped by a mink throw; built-in bedside tables have smoked Lucite drawers. Andy Warhol's Oxidation painting, created by urinating on copper-based paint, was hung over the bed. Two 1970s French chairs upholstered in goatskin converse with a pair of Italian Baroque tables. Picasso's *Femme Assise* observes the proceedings.

The penthouse, originally a rooftop shack, was rebuilt as a modernist pavilion overlooking a garden terrace. Used as a media and billiard room by the family, it is also a favored site for cocktail parties and barbecues. The interior is wallpapered in Warhol portraits and appointed with twentieth-century furnishings, including a teddy-bear-mohair banquette, making for a comfortable retreat.

Georgis-designed Centrifuge mohair sofa and coffee table in steel and limestone, Louis XV chandelier, custom Ink Splatter rug, Franz Kline painting, and Jeff Koons sculptures in the living room

With design, there are various pails to pick from to create an inspired mix. One pail might be Asian decorative arts (Coromandel, jade, Chinese furniture, Japanese lacquer), another is animal prints (zebra, jaguar, cougar, bear), another is twentieth-century furnishings (resin, chrome, Plexi), and another is eighteenth-century Europe (Louis XVI architectural furniture, eccentric English pieces). You pull something from each of those pails and you make magic.

ABOVE
Dining room with rosewood-and-stainless-steel table by Georgis, Marc Newson Komed chairs, Louis XV chandelier, Paula Hayes terrarium, and Richard Serra drawing

OPPOSITE
Living room with painting by Cy Twombly

Make It Fabulous

BELOW
Master bedroom with rug and
stainless-steel-and-Plexiglas bed
and bedside table by Georgis and
Andy Warhol Oxidation painting

OPPOSITE
Limestone fireplace, goatskin-
upholstered chairs from the 1970s,
cast-glass-and-Plexiglas low table
by Georgis, Italian Baroque table,
Felix Agostini sconces, and Picasso
painting in master bedroom

LEFT
Ebonized-oak library with
mirrored ceiling, Sciolari stainless-
steel chandelier, button-tufted
Chesterfield sofa by Georgis,
anthracite side tables, pen-shell
coffee table, pair of Carlo Bugatti
chairs, black rabbit rug, chainmail
stainless-steel curtains, and
Damien Hirst medicine cabinet

ABOVE
Library detail with Jean Royère
chairs and collection of crystals and
specimens

ABOVE
Lava-stone-and-stainless-steel
coffee table, teddy-bear-mohair
sofa, 1970s Italian chair, and
collection of Andy Warhol portraits
in the penthouse

RIGHT
Penthouse with teak deck, trellis,
and pergola, stainless-steel
planters, seating area, and Paolo
Soleri bronze bells

Summer Residence

Watermill, New York
2005

Aligned in the Sand. *Georgis designed this 4,600-square-foot, three-bedroom summer residence as a two-story, cedar-clad rectangular volume fronting on a landscaped auto court. The main entry to the house, reached by a shallow ramp, is tucked behind a long, high, vine-covered masonry wall. While the front of the house is closed, protected by several layers of landscape and walls, the back is open, featuring a balcony and, on the ground floor, large sliding glass doors facing a paved pool terrace. A cabana is placed within a thick garden wall, and steps lead down to a garden and Burnett's Creek. Inside, the house has an open plan with a two-story living room at one end and a kitchen and service area at the other. The interior is decorated with a mix of vintage and custom pieces, including paper light fixtures by Isamu Noguchi customized with black ink drips by Georgis. The house also features contemporary artworks in vivid color palettes. The extensive landscaping scheme was designed by Paula Hayes.*

This house was built for a dear friend starting a new chapter of her life. I wanted to create a place that would nurture and protect her. We had worked together on urban projects, and for this newly built residence she wanted to be able to live casually and informally with her children. Like many of my clients—and like myself—she is a great admirer of modern architecture and design and collects contemporary art.

We transformed a small guesthouse at the entry to the site into a gate house. The structure and a treillaged wall built in front of it were painted green to recede into the landscape. Adequate parking is a perennial problem in this area, and so we created a large rectangular auto court paved in refined pea gravel that accommodates parking at one side. The house itself is a modernist cedar box behind an opaque "fortified" wall fronting the auto court and parallel to the street.

Landscape artist Paula Hayes alleviated the severe gravel-paved court with a lush island planted with a magnificent Japanese maple tree. The vegetated island humanizes the court and tempers its scale. It also converts the fortified wall, covered in ivy and underplanted with junipers, into a garden wall, making the house seem even more concealed and protected. To one side of the site are beds of flowering lavender; to the other, a newly created wildflower meadow.

The interior of the house is open in plan, with contiguous living, dining, family, and kitchen areas. (The kitchen can be closed off from the other rooms.) These spaces have sliding doors that open up to a beautiful creek and Mecox Bay beyond. In the summer, the interior rooms and the pool terrace offer a single indoor-outdoor living space. The section is more complex with a double-height living room, skylights, and a secret garden off the dining area between the cedar shell of the house and the fortified wall.

The interior design was intended to be minimal and luminous throughout. The furniture is designed for comfort with a luxe beach quality. Finishes are light and simple, in keeping with the ambience: crisp white walls, bleached-ash floors, open-weave linen sheers.

In the living room, a classic palette of navy and white, with a pale silver-blue silk rug, relates to the nearby ocean. A sculptural fireplace separates the living space from the dining area and creates two seating areas for conversation. I furnished the space with classic modern polished-chrome chairs by Milo Baughman covered in white leather and horsehair, a pair of Japanese lacquered occasional tables by Maison Jansen, and two three-tiered occasional tables by Sakim from the 1950s. At the end of the room is a custom cast-glass coffee table and a marvelously deep Belgian linen sofa strewn with a multitude of blue-and-white-patterned pillows. A low navy-linen backless chaise curves around the fireplace to create another seating group. Peter Zimmermann's poured-epoxy painting and Noguchi lanterns that I stained with ink add color, style, and whimsy to the living room.

In the dining room, I paired an English-elm plank table with an antler chandelier and Edwardian silver hurricane candles—an unexpected but felicitous combination. A floating teak screen, which also contains bookshelves, separates the dining area from the family room. The family room has a mix of rustic and refined furnishings: coarse hemp matting, a chocolate-brown Belgian linen sofa, polished-stainless-steel swivel chairs, and a Corian-topped coffee table. I love contrasting rough and fine things to coax out their essences.

On the second floor, a suite of two children's rooms and a playroom opens onto an exterior balcony. The children can use a floating stair from the balcony to the pool terrace to come and go to their bedrooms. The master suite at the end of the house has views of the creek and a Juliet balcony that allows the client to observe the living room from above. The back of the house is an homage to midcentury Southern California design, with large sliding glass doors, cantilevered balconies, and outdoor lounging, dining, and kitchen all overlooking the pool and creek.

Plan, First Floor

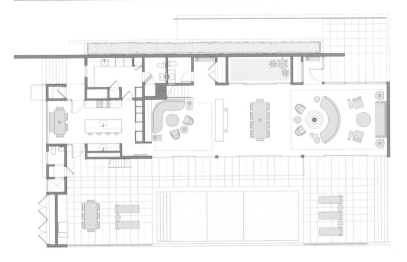

0 4 8

Plan, Second Floor

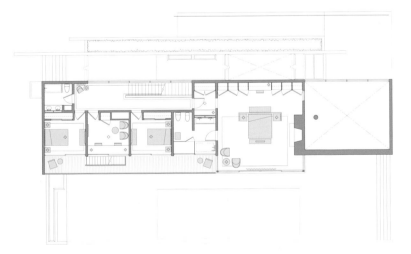

PAGE 107
View from pool terrace to dining and family rooms on main level and bedrooms above

OPPOSITE
Exterior view of living room

OVERLEAF
Cedar-clad entry facade with ivy-covered wall with entry ramp; the garden was designed by Paula Hayes

Over time I have become less likely to design open-plan houses. While I love the fluidity of space and the opportunity to modulate it in an abstract way, I find them challenging to inhabit in terms of acoustics, privacy, and decoration. In an open-plan house, sound travels, privacy is hard to achieve, and there's no place to change color or wall treatment. In my Manhattan townhouse, there are moments when I think, "Oh, wouldn't it be great if we could do a red-silk-velvet upholstered room?" But there's no way to start and stop the velvet because the walls are continuous throughout the building. There's one paint color and that's it.

ABOVE
Dining room with English-elm-and-stainless-steel table by Georgis, Italian stainless-steel-and-leather chairs, and antler chandelier

OPPOSITE
Living room with Noguchi lanterns (inked by Georgis), white linen sofa, Milo Baughman chairs, three-tiered Sakim side tables, and Peter Zimmermann painting

ABOVE
Entry with stainless-steel-and-lacquer trestle table and Baughman scoop chair

RIGHT
Kitchen with cerused-oak cabinets, stainless-steel counter, terrazzo floors, walnut table, Dorothy Schindele chairs, Stilnovo pendant fixture, and view to bamboo garden

Make It Fabulous

BELOW
Brown linen sofa by Georgis, T. H. Robsjohn-Gibbings side tables, Milo Baughman chairs, coral-stone lamps, and hemp rug in the family room

OPPOSITE
Master bedroom with Georgis-designed oak headboard, Karl Springer stainless-steel bedside table, and 1960s American plaster lamp

Chinatown Brasserie
New York, New York
2006

Film Set for Dining. *Georgis designed this two-story, 11,200-square-foot bar and restaurant as a Chinese-themed stage set. It is located in a late-1880s building designed by Henry Hardenbergh in Manhattan's East Village. At the center of the upper, street-level floor sits a large open dining space lined with booths; surrounding it are a bar, enclosed private dining rooms, and a traditional Chinese garden complete with a moon gate. Another bar and a lounge are located on the lower level; the connecting stairway is adjacent to the main entrance and lands next to a koi pond surrounded by bronze mirrors. The decoration mixes real Chinese antiques and Chinoiserie, including Georgis's custom-designed lanterns—enlarged versions of one he found in an antiques shop—and hand-painted floral wallpapers by Gracie in New York City. Georgis developed numerous fixtures for the interior, including backlit antique mirror panels and a hammered-zinc top for the bar. Georgis also commissioned works by several artists, including paintings by Robert Kushner and large ceramic sutra holders by Peter Lane.*

When the client approached me, the idea of the restaurant was already set: a brasserie showcasing the cuisine of China, including dim sum, in a large space on Lafayette Street in Manhattan. Enormous hospitality spaces are always challenging and this was no exception. The client was concerned about the scale and wanted to be able to shut down portions of the restaurant at off-peak hours. Stylistically, the owner wanted the restaurant to have the patina of age, similar to Balthazar, a successful New York bistro that seems like it is much older than its fifteen years.

My first decision was to insert a grand stair from the street-level main floor to the lower-level club. A bridge across the large stair opening, with a koi pond below, gives access to the restaurant on the main level. The dining room, ringed by banquettes based on the design of opium beds, is at the center of the almost square space; the long rectangular areas on either side accommodate a bar and additional dining room. Dividing the plan into discrete areas allowed for more intimately scaled spaces, and at off-peak hours it is easy to close off one of the dining zones. On the bar side is a vestibule with a little Chinese garden that leads to an upper, private dining area. Lighting was also used to scale down the space and create a sense of intimacy.

In many respects, the inspiration for the restaurant was Hollywood, and Hollywood's idea of China. The client wanted something that looked old; I wanted something very theatrical and scenographic. I have always been intrigued by the 1941 movie *The Shanghai Gesture*. Josef von Sternberg's film takes place in a casino (in the original play, it was a brothel) with insanely fantastical interiors. Their authenticity,

or lack thereof, was not what interested me—instead I was inspired by the Hollywood conception of decadent Shanghai. In one scene a feast is held in an incredible banquet room with spectacular murals painted by the Chinese-born artist Keye Luke (who became a Hollywood actor). It was the feel and look of that movie that influenced me—I thought we should do something here that would be almost hallucinogenic.

At the same time I was inspired by a genuine appreciation of Chinese architecture, gardens, and decorative arts. Antique and contemporary books on Chinese residential architecture and gardens in my own library provided important references for detailing the space. I like to think that the bridge with a Chinese-fretwork-patterned railing, screens with a cracked-ice pattern, and a round Chinese moon gate framing a garden view are all respectful interpretations of historic precedents.

For the decorative arts, Chinese models were also valuable sources. Banquettes and paneling utilize Ming Dynasty furniture details; hand-painted wallpaper, by Gracie, is based on eighteenth-century export wallpaper. Portière panels made from rich Chinese silks separate the central dining room from adjacent spaces. Custom lanterns were based on Chinese prototypes, and Chinese ceramics accessorize the space. I also commissioned two large paintings from Robert Kushner, who has a strong interest in Chinese painting.

This theatrical approach may not be appropriate in an apartment or house. But in a restaurant, where guests come for a short time, the expectations are different—they want to be transported to another world.

Plan, Lower Floor

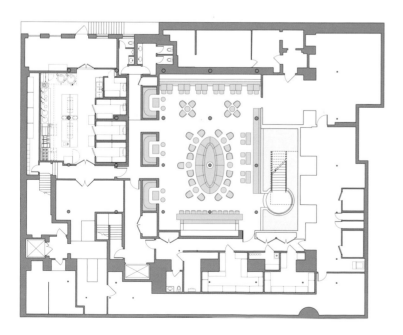

Plan, Main Floor

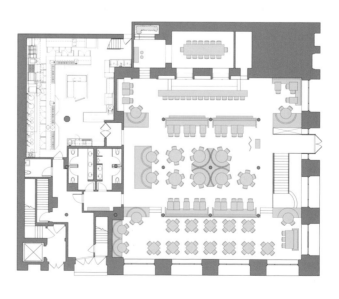

0   8   16

PAGE 118
Upper dining room with bamboo-paneled ceiling, stenciled walls, silk lanterns, and Robert Kushner painting

ABOVE
Entrance with custom black-lacquer and hand-painted Gracie-wallpaper reception desk flanked by Chinese portière panels

ABOVE
Bar dining room with banquette,
Chinese moon gate to upper-level
private dining room, painting by
Robert Kushner, and ceramic sutra
holder by Peter Lane

ABOVE
Bar with hammered-zinc top, vintage Chinese photographs, and silk lanterns

OVERLEAF
Dining room with circular oxblood leather banquettes, opium-bed-inspired banquettes at the perimeter, and silk Chinese lanterns

Apartment, 2008: Georgis-designed Macassar dining table with rubbed lacquered-linen "placemats," velvet Lotus chairs, and wool-and-silk Rorschach rug in dining room

Furniture Fetish

Residence, Los Angeles, c. 1952: Living room by interior designer Billy Haines and architect A. Quincy Jones

While William Georgis conceives his furnishings as parts of a *Gesamtkunstwerk*—an integrated ensemble of architecture, interior design, and decoration—his custom-designed furniture, rugs, curtains, wallpaper, and hardware command their own attention. Like his architecture and interiors, Georgis's fittings and furnishings look to precedents both global and historic. They too are designed to the most minute detail and mix luxurious and unexpected materials with strong, geometric forms, setting up dialogues both within and between individual pieces.

Georgis adopts varying strategies to incorporate furnishings into his interiors. Sometimes he uses them to reinforce the architecture, such as the gridded rugs in the Lever House lobby that mirror the building's metal-and-glass curtain wall and borrow their color from the glass spandrels. Other times, he uses furnishings to challenge the settings. His playful mix of custom pieces with antiques from Europe, Africa, and Asia in a Colonial Revival beach house in Southampton produces an effect that is "distinctly non-chintzy," he notes, "kind of unexpected behind the staid historicist exterior. This is just what the client wanted: a house that represented his unconventional attitude."

Georgis's custom pieces might be generated by necessity: when he can't find the right bedside table in the marketplace, for example, he designs a version that is tricked out with hidden doors and shelves. Or they might be inspired by clients' social imperatives: they require a modular dining room table that can accommodate both intimate events and large gatherings in multiple configurations. Often, though, they are brought about by an aesthetic impulse to create distinct signature pieces, such as a circular sofa or an ink-splattered rug. These give Georgis the most artistic license, and he pulls from a grab bag of historical and geographic sources for their design and manufacture: Chinese Ming Dynasty furnishings, Japanese decorative arts of the Edo period, African sculpture, eighteenth-century French decorative arts, even contemporary popular culture. His references for custom rugs have included a spin-art postcard from SeaWorld and wrapping paper from Tokyo's Mitsukoshi department store. As in his interior designs, Georgis uses traditional tropes and age-old finishes in new contexts, as well as exotic materials in unusual ways, often creating objects that are surprising, beautiful, and, in themselves, works of art. Georgis also often collaborates with artists, such as Jeff Zimmerman, who create unique furnishings for his interiors.

Just as Georgis acknowledges the role of clients in sparking his designs, he also credits a coterie of

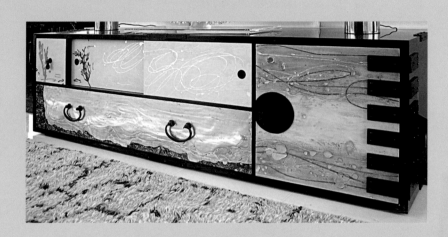

OPPOSITE, CLOCKWISE FROM TOP

*Stiletto stool with zebra silk velvet, orange silk satin, and nickel;
Emily chair in stainless steel and canvas; channel-tufted leather sofa;
Persian-lamb tabouret with antique mirrored legs and three-tiered
bronze table with copper enamel*

ABOVE, CLOCKWISE FROM TOP LEFT

*Wenge cabinet with lacquered interior;
armoire with gold-and-asphalt-églomisé doors; bronze commode
with Gracie-decorated doors; tansu decorated by Nancy Lorenz;
two views of black-lacquer cabinet with antique Chinese hardstone
panels depicting flora; blackened-steel commode with
gold-and-asphalt-églomisé doors; Macassar-and-parchment armoire
with bronze handles by Michele Oka Doner*

Residence, 2009: Dining room with fiberglass Two-In-One dining table composed of two circular tables with hourglass-shaped bridge

Apartment, 2008: Living room with linen-velvet Centrifuge sofa with walnut legs; coffee tables in gouged aluminum, white glass, and glass rods; Spin Art rug in wool and silk

artisans in realizing them. Many trace their crafts back centuries, expertly deploying such techniques as verre églomisé, a pre-Roman process of gilding the back side of glass that was repopularized in eighteenth-century France, or mercury gilding for mirrors, which provides a richer effect than the standard reflective surface.

Premier among Georgis's collaborators is V'Soske, a New York–based company that hand-weaves tapestry-quality rugs. Massachusetts-based Bruce Volz and Tony Clarke, furniture designers and makers, operate in the eighteenth-century aristocratic tradition of the *ensemblier*. They orchestrate the teams of artisans required to make Georgis's custom pieces, which can include a variety of crafts, from woodwork and metalwork to parchment application, decorative wood carving, lacquering, and upholstering with exotic animal skins like skunk and mink. For his interiors, Georgis designs even the smallest details, including architectural hardware that is painstakingly fabricated by E. R. Butler and P. E. Guerin. He also occasionally crafts his own pieces, dripping ink on Noguchi paper lanterns for a Long Island beach house when he needed "something really big" for the double-height living room.

Georgis's repertoire includes hand-painted wallpapers produced by Gracie, a dealer in antique Chinese wallpapers founded in 1898. The company now has two studios, one staffed by painters trained in the classical Chinese tradition, the other by Japanese artists. "I like to go to them with my own

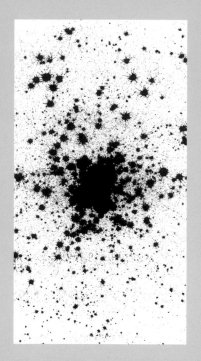

CLOCKWISE FROM TOP LEFT
Cartoons for Blood Splatter rug, Ink Splatter rug, Color Splatter rug, Rorschach rug, Spin Art rug

TOP ROW
*Fiberglass-and-teak console; bronze guéridon table with
bone-inlaid shagreen top; black-glass-and-brass coffee table*

SECOND ROW
*Guéridon desk in cerused oak with vitrine drawer; stainless-steel
coffee table with copper-enamel top; cast-glass console*

THIRD ROW
*Cast-glass-topped coffee table with honeycomb ceramic base
by Peter Lane; bronze Diamond Set dining table with
white-gold-leaf-and-lacquer top; dining table with top of Cold Spring
granite and ebonized oak*

CLOCKWISE FROM TOP LEFT

Diamond Set coffee table in blackened steel and limestone; Waterfall coffee table in bronze with birch-bark ceramic top by Peter Lane; bronze-trimmed anigre bed with attached bedside table in parchment with stiletto leg; white-leather-wrapped stainless-steel bedside table; stainless-steel-and-smoked-Plexiglas bedside table; bedside table in parchment with nickel stiletto leg

CLOCKWISE FROM TOP LEFT
Nickel-and-glass-rod sconce; sconce with Japanese-tea-ceremony ceramic tile; bronze easel lamp with onyx; cast-glass key stand; two views of cast-glass-and-nickel retractable console; Georgis-made paper lanterns

ideas and say, 'Let's interpret them using the kind of academic background you have,'" Georgis says. For his design of a pair of cabinets for a Park Avenue living room, for instance, "I told Gracie, 'Let's do something with butterflies on a gold background with grasses.' I sent my sketch to Gracie's Japanese studio, and they came back with full-blown cartoons. Then they made samples, and so on." Gracie's hand-painted wallpapers also add notes of authenticity to Chinatown Brasserie.

By focusing his attention on custom furnishings as part of an interior ensemble, Georgis operates within a tradition that stretches back to eighteenth-century designer-craftsmen in the service of the French court—and earlier—and continues in the work of such twentieth-century masters as Emile-Jacques Ruhlmann, Jean-Michel Frank, Billy Haines, and Maison Jansen. Their furnishings are now studied by scholars and prized by collectors as works of art in themselves, outside of their architectural contexts—just as Georgis's works may be one day. Georgis is intimately familiar with these predecessors, steeping himself through deep research not only in the history of furniture forms but in the complex techniques of their execution. As a result, his furnishings have strong associative resonances that add to the formal and emotional richness of his interiors.

D.A. and N.S.

Palm Beach Apartment
Palm Beach, Florida
2006

Island Fever. *This 3,600-square-foot, three-bedroom apartment in Palm Beach, Florida, is organized around panoramic views of the Atlantic Ocean to the east and Lake Worth Lagoon to the west. The living room and master suite overlook the ocean, and the pool room and guest suites have a view of the lagoon. The dining room, kitchen, and bathrooms occupy interior locations. Georgis focused on creating an interior of vivid color—coral and emerald green, for example—with references to South Florida nature and culture and also to playful resort architecture in general. The eclectic mix of furnishings ranges from modernist classics by Eero Saarinen and Charles and Ray Eames to more exotic elements, such as Chinese-seagrass-patterned rugs in the living room, dining room, and guest bedroom; zebra-patterned wallpaper in the billiards room; and a bamboo-framed dining table. For the 510-square-foot poolside cabana, Georgis used Martinique banana-leaf wallpaper—best known from the Beverly Hills Hotel—and monkey imagery, a witty homage to a favorite Palm Beach motif.*

Make It Fabulous

This was my third project for these clients. Their two New York apartments, in comparison, were elegant and restrained; for this apartment, in a new condominium in Palm Beach, it was time for some fun. My clients understand the cultural and aesthetic extremes of Palm Beach, a community they love. We decided to approach the project from a position of respect *and* irony, to exercise our appreciation of the absurd.

Palm Beach has a sense of fantasy not seen elsewhere. Great architects like Addison Mizner, Maurice Fatio, and Joseph Urban imbued the skinny barrier island with a tropical glamour reminiscent of classic Hollywood movie sets. Renaissance, Spanish, Arabic, and Chinese influences were liberally mixed into heady cocktails, mélanges of styles I find intoxicating.

The apartment is located on a low floor, offering a vantage similar to an ocean liner's deck. I made some minor changes to the plan and otherwise limited our architectural interventions to installing driftwood-colored oak floors. The project was to be about decor.

The entrance foyer is based on an irresistible cliché—the blue of Tiffany boxes. This particular shade of turquoise is spectacular in subtropical light and provides a luminous backdrop for Chinese export blue-and-white lamps, silver-plated shell-shaped brackets supporting dark turquoise foo dogs, and a white-laminate Pierre Cardin commode. The concatenation is cacophonous—the blues vibrate in proximity.

The clients requested an informal living room where they could lounge casually, entertain, and watch television. Rather than resort to the common strategy of hiding the television, I embraced it. I created a room arranged around a twenty-one-foot-long sofa with two large ottomans in the middle, which form an enormous queen-bed-size sofa, the perfect locale for television viewing of old movies, sporting events, and the Rose Bowl parade. Two seating groups, made up of Eames and Baughman lounge chairs, vintage travertine-topped tables, and wicker poufs, are arranged on either side of the ottomans. A suite of irreverent drawings by David Kramer, a school of nine yellow goldfish, Hawaiian appliqué pillows, and Noguchi lanterns provide character, color, and high style.

While the living room palette is fairly neutral, the adjacent dining room is a riot of color. I love juxtaposing disparate spaces: small next to large, neutral next to color-saturated. The space doesn't have windows, so it made perfect sense to create a fantastical garden. Thibaut's classic Flora wallpaper provides a lush backdrop of exotic flowers for Charles Hollis Jones's Plexiglas chairs covered in green cotton velvet. A dining table with a bamboo base and glass top reflects a stainless-steel-beribboned chandelier. Mirrors create ecstasy through repetition—a Baroque trick. Nothing succeeds like excess, as Oscar Wilde once said.

I associate pool rooms with rich materials, liquor, and questionable behavior. Why should this room be any different? It is possible to exceed expectation and simultaneously subvert tradition. Zebra wallpaper replaces the expected wood paneling, referencing Gino's restaurant in Manhattan and the banquettes of the El Morocco Club. An antique pool table is covered in cerulean baize rather than tournament green. A bar tray and two onyx lamps are arranged on a parchment commode. The setting sun bounces golden light off Lake Worth Lagoon and into the room, the ideal finishing touch.

I often find myself returning to a pale and calming palette for bedrooms—blues, greens, silvers. This master bedroom is no exception, but I also introduced shots of vivid color and furniture with strong character to stop the room from washing away to sea. Chinese pieces, including a fretwork bed, bedside tables, and 1950s figural pewter lamps from Hong Kong, are mixed with a Vladimir Kagan chaise, Emilio Pucci fabric–covered chairs, and a majolica faux-bois floor lamp. The room maintains its serenity while sporting an edge.

A poolside cabana is essential for Palm Beach living, and my clients were delighted to learn that one was included with their apartment. Reference in decorating is a powerful tool, and in this case I used the famous banana-leaf wallpaper from the Beverly Hills Hotel to conjure a storied resort of a certain period. It also provides a lush and colorful backdrop for vintage Paul Frankl rattan furniture, a Chinoiserie commode, a zebra-upholstered chair, and monkeys galore. There are monkey lamps and a collection of Monchhichi stuffed animals from the 1970s. Monkeys everywhere, which is very Palm Beach.

Plan

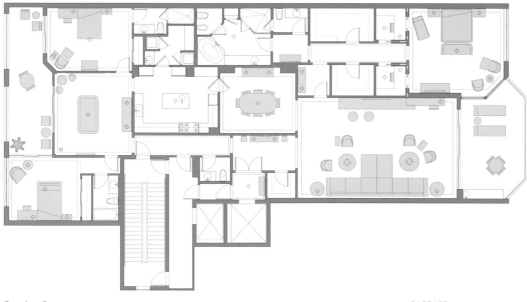

0 4 8

PAGE 137
Cabana with Martinique wallpaper (originally designed for the Beverly Hills Hotel), monkey collection, John Stewart X-frame desk, and zebra-skin-clad Milo Baughman chrome chair

OPPOSITE
Dining room with gilt keystone-shaped mirrors, Thibaut Barbados wallpaper, white-lacquer credenza, plaster turtle lamps, and Charles Hollis Jones green velvet chairs

It's great to have spaces with different characters. Certain palaces have under one roof a variety of styles that more or less relate to each other, but then there's something from left field. Think of Chantilly's Grande Singerie, which is decorated with paintings of monkeys. It's screwball, it's sudden—it's kind of a fabulous moment. You gasp, "My God!" I like to create a background and then do something off base. It seems to have more power that way.

ABOVE
Guest room with vintage green-and-white armoire, rattan chaise, and shell mirror

RIGHT
Paul Frankl rattan-and-canvas furniture, Plexiglas waterfall table, and Chinese figural wood lamp in cabana

PREVIOUS PAGES
Living room with Eames lounge
chairs, sofa with Hawaiian quilted
pillows, James Mont coffee table,
seagrass rug, and view to the
Atlantic Ocean

ABOVE
Tiffany-blue foyer with silvered-shell
wall brackets, Chinese foo dogs,
Pierre Cardin credenza, and blue-
and-white lamps

OPPOSITE
Pool room with parchment
credenza, onyx lamps, and zebra
wallpaper

144

East Quogue Residence

East Quogue, New York
2007

Sea Worthy. *This six-bedroom, 6,600-square-foot summer house, on a spit of land between Shinnecock Bay and the Atlantic Ocean in East Quogue, takes advantage of both bay and ocean views. The rectangular structure, a two-story volume of ebonized mahogany with shotcrete end walls, is offset by two circular forms—one supporting an exterior spiral stair, the other housing a powder room and outdoor fireplace at the upper level. The house is raised on concrete fins to comply with environmental regulations. A long floating ramp with a glass railing provides access to the main entry. The upper level is treated as a piano nobile: the open living, dining, and kitchen areas expand onto an ocean-side deck; a two-story entry/stairhall separates the living spaces from the master suite. The swimming pool, also located on the upper level, is treated as a separate volume; a wide bridge to the pool—in effect, a terrace—has a frosted-glass-panel floor that allows natural light into the bedrooms on the lower level. Many of the house's furnishings were designed by Georgis.*

This is one of the more adventurous projects I've worked on. The clients' program, which called for a swimming pool on the house's upper level, necessitated unusual solutions and prompted unorthodox results. The house is situated on a razor-thin barrier island wedged between Shinnecock Bay and the Atlantic Ocean. The delicate terrain is subject to flooding; to satisfy code requirements, we built the house on a series of concrete fins so that the sea could surge beneath.

The severity of the box is tempered by episodic design features: a nautically inspired ramp leads to the front door; a stucco drum at the back (reminiscent of the air vent of an ocean liner) houses a powder room, barbecue, and fireplace; and an exterior stair that connects the two floors is cantilevered from a Cor-ten steel cylinder that holds an outdoor shower. I've always been enamored of the way Le Corbusier used programmatic and circulation elements as dramatic means to break up a box; his influence is unmistakable in these elements, which both animate the house and allow it to function. Materials also enrich the otherwise austere box. The roof is terne-coated stainless steel, and the cladding and windows are ebonized mahogany.

An entry hall, children's bedrooms, guest suite, and staff quarters occupy the first floor and enjoy expansive views of Shinnecock Bay. The living and dining area and master bedroom suite overlook spectacular ocean and bay vistas on the level above. Because the clients wanted to install a swimming pool on the upper floor, between the house and the ocean, a separate volume (also raised on concrete fin walls) is pulled away from the house to admit light to the lower level. An acid-etched glass deck connects the house and pool; at night, lit from beneath, it makes a magical impression.

The interior design is summery and casual. The double-height entrance hall features custom-designed armoires with asphalt-drip-and-gilded-verre-églomisé doors executed from my paintings, a Chinese console, a Bigert & Bergström hanging sculpture, and Massimo Vitali photographs. The stair is fabricated from thick plates of steel with a leather-wrapped handrail.

The living and dining areas occupy a loftlike space with water views on two sides. A custom walnut-and-stainless-steel dining table and an enormous Richard Misrach photograph of the ocean anchor the dining area. In the living area is a large sofa with walnut ribs reminiscent of boat construction, Sarah Hobbs's photograph *Untitled (Corks)*, and an Hervé Van der Straeten table.

Le Corbusier said, "The house is a machine for living in" and advocated open-plan houses raised on pilotis and unencumbered by load-bearing walls. For me, Corbusier's strategy suggested a way to build in an environmentally sensitive area that would satisfy clients who desired open spaces visually connected to expansive vistas. I like to think that the design of the house is inevitable—as if the design were predestined given the manner in which people like to live by the sea.

Plan, First Floor

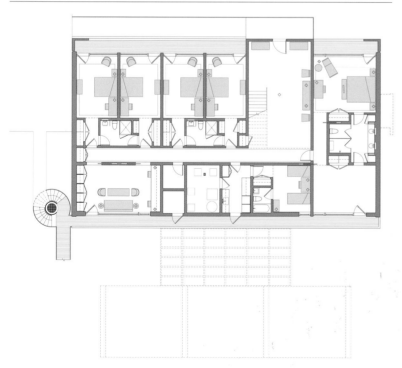

Plan, Second Floor

PAGE 146
Upper and lower decks connected by Cor-ten steel stair wrapping around outdoor shower

OPPOSITE TOP
Front facade (facing Shinnecock Bay)

OPPOSITE BOTTOM
Oceanside facade

OVERLEAF
Oceanside facade with elevated swimming pool

0   6   12

LEFT
Double-height entrance foyer with
steel-plate staircase, pickled-ash
floors, and pair of Georgis-designed
gold-and-asphalt-églomisé
armoires

ABOVE
Chinese console, wingback chairs,
photographs by Massimo Vitali,
and hanging sculpture by Bigert &
Bergström in entrance foyer

PREVIOUS PAGES
Dining and living areas with walnut-and-stainless-steel dining table by Georgis and photograph by Richard Misrach; the custom Whalebone sofa defines a seating area

ABOVE
Master bedroom with shotcrete walls, burl-maple bed and bedside tables by Georgis, Peter Lane lamps, Jens Risom chair, Shizue Imai ceramic sculpture, and photographs by Martina Mullaney

ABOVE
View into main-level lounge area
and lower-level gym

building completed in 2006, was decorated by Georgis. His architectural interventions create a series of defined spaces for the public areas of the 2,700-square-foot, two-bedroom loft. The main public areas—foyer, dining, living—are arrayed along the perimeter wall, composed almost entirely of floor-to-ceiling windows. Tucked in a corner next to the living space is a wood-paneled study; the master suite, at the opposite end of the loft, is separated from the public areas by a private hallway. The bathrooms and kitchen are located opposite the main public rooms. Furnishings include pieces designed by Georgis; collaborations between Georgis and such artists as Nancy Lorenz, Peter Lane, and Michele Oka Doner; and vintage pieces by Emile-Jacques Ruhlmann, Paul Frankl, and George Nakashima. These are juxtaposed with works from the clients' art collection, including pieces by John Chamberlain, Joan Mitchell, Andy Warhol, and Kenny Scharf. Finishes include walnut walls and rose-colored sheer curtains.

The word mix *is used repeatedly in discussions of interior design, and its importance cannot be overestimated. Each piece of art or furniture possesses an inherent character, culture, and value. When two objects from different periods and cultures are juxtaposed, magic can happen. For instance, in the library an eccentric nineteenth-century English side table with a base consisting of a bronze Cavalier King Charles spaniel atop an eagle, a leather Chesterfield sofa, a contemporary coffee table with a ceramic top, and an Abstract Expressionist collage by Franz Kline inhabit the same space. While the side table and sofa might be expected bedfellows in a conventional English interior, the rusticity of the ceramic tabletop and the bold gesture of the Kline collage create a new context. The objects relate visually, not historically. A certain frisson ensues, and that frisson is the magic of my profession.*

Foyer with suede-covered French armchairs, cast-glass-and-ceramic coffee table by Georgis and Peter Lane, and John Chamberlain sculpture

ABOVE
Living room with George Nakashima
chairs, Philippe Hiquily side table,
French glass-and-brass coffee table,
and French daybed

ABOVE
Master bedroom with gold-leaf-and-
resin-drip screen by Nancy Lorenz,
rosewood commode, and Anton Henning
painting

OVERLEAF
Library with ceramic-and-bronze
coffee table by Georgis and Peter Lane,
Chesterfield sofa, Fortuny-covered
armchairs, and Andy Warhol painting;
the doorway leads to the living room

American Hospital of Paris 2003 International Designer Showhouse, New York: Bedroom for an imaginary deranged woman with mirrored ceiling; black moiré walls, carpet, rabbit fur, and rubber coverlet; and painting by Otto Zitko

Subversive Intent

Jean-François Daigre residence, Paris, 1970s: Louis XIV–style mirrored room designed by Valerian Rybar

Designs that are surreal and transgressive, from a Louis XIV–style mirrored room decorated with Ultrasuede to a pair of black velvet gloves with knife-sharp gold fingernails, are touchstones for William Georgis. Their creators—Valerian Rybar and Elsa Schiaparelli, respectively—are masters of subversive intent, an attitude and design strategy that figures prominently in Georgis's own work. Georgis admits, "I love to shock"—an aesthetic trademark that many of his clients admire. Risk-takers themselves, they share with Georgis an appreciation of the outré and the macabre—one patron speaks admiringly of Georgis's use of "emotional and sexual images, materials you would find in a brothel, and his desire to take an architectural feature or a material and do something different with it." This interest in an aesthetic that challenges the norms shapes his clients' environments as well as the art they collect. Works by artists such as Richard Prince, George Condo, Mike Kelley, and Damien Hirst, who appropriate and subvert artistic, cultural, and social traditions, figure prominently in many of Georgis's projects.

To subvert, of course, requires context. Georgis considers his education at Princeton University and wide-ranging discussions there about approaches to history—a key topic of postmodernist thought in the early 1980s—to be important grounding for his current work. "How do you deal with context?" Georgis asks. "Do you just imitate it? That's not good enough, really. I think you've got to confront it, manipulate it, twist it to say something fresh."

Georgis adopts a range of approaches to history—from respect through selective contextualism and juxtaposition to transgression. The strategy he chooses depends on a number of factors: the quality and integrity of the existing structure, the client's preferences—some want to preserve, some want to remove historic detail—and Georgis's own aesthetic impulses. His careful restoration of Lever House's public spaces, for instance, demonstrates his esteem for this mid-twentieth-century masterpiece. For other projects he mixes new with old, noting that "what's always been interesting is to be able to juxtapose the new with the familiar and to create an unsettling alternative that maybe hasn't been seen before or is revisited—a kind of frisson."

Georgis does this in his architecture as well as in his decoration. Behind the masonry walls of the venerable Carlyle Hotel, he developed a startlingly "super-minimalist" apartment. It is even more surprising in relation to the aggressively retro interiors of the public spaces, designed by Thierry Despont. In Georgis's own New York living room, a disco ball, symbol of the louche seventies he so admires, floats above decorative objects like

Soho Loft, New York, 2005: Guest bedroom in a glass bubble; voyeuristic relationship between master bedroom and bathroom

This project, simply put, is about art. The client inhabits the center of the New York art world, collecting postwar and contemporary art, befriending artists, and commissioning site-specific works. So my mandate was to create an appropriate setting for an ever-expanding art collection, but also to create a home, not a gallery. Since all of this had to be accomplished with minimal architectural intervention in a newly constructed apartment building, I focused on finishes and furnishings to play with the scale of the spaces and to provide a flexible backdrop for the client's collection while also accommodating his living and entertaining needs. I designed and selected furnishings that could hold their own with the dramatic paintings and sculptures, but basically the interiors are quiet and discreet—the art is more edgy than the decor.

An important aspect of the work here was to develop the right wall finish for the main areas. I wanted to provide a neutral background for the changing artwork, but also a distinctive treatment that would distinguish the rooms from a commercial gallery with its generic gypsum-board walls. In our earliest discussion about finishes, I told the client, "Everybody who collects contemporary art wants flat white walls. Why don't we make textured walls and hang the art from picture rails so we don't destroy the walls every time you move something?" I developed a striated resin with integral color and a matte finish that has the quality of plaster—the effect is sublime.

The double-height living and dining areas enjoy spectacular views over Gramercy Park. To differentiate living from dining, I designed an L-shaped sofa with a built-in shelf at its back and placed it on a custom wool-and-silk rug. A Yutaka Sone sculpture of a Los Angeles freeway interchange carved in white marble is used as the base for a coffee table; an attenuated Murano chandelier mediates the scale of the space. Paintings by Christopher Wool and sculptures by Claes Oldenburg mix with furnishings by Royère and Le Corbusier. In the dining area, Warhol's twelve Mona Lisas preside over a dining table fabricated from ebonized oak and black granite and accompanied by Richard Neutra dining chairs. The subtle palette—black, white, and gray—allows the art to be the dominant voice in the room.

The library and study, adjacent to the living room, needed to be masculine for my bachelor client. Dark finishes are a great way to make small rooms seem larger, since in dark rooms it is difficult to discern the perimeter. So I paneled the walls in wenge. I took a cue from Paul Rudolph to deal with the low ceilings: a large mirror-top table bounces light up to the ceiling and takes the floor out of the room like a centrifuge carnival ride. It's the opposite of a mirrored ceiling. (Another trick is to use a high-gloss paint on the ceiling to turn it into a reflective surface.) Robert Mapplethorpe photographs, an Alexander Calder sculpture, and a custom-designed, 1970s-inspired suede sectional sofa with sheepskin pillows complete the picture.

Dark bedrooms are very comforting—sleeping in them is like sleeping inside a cave or a womb. Upholstered walls, which provide coddling and acoustical privacy, are even better. So I was thrilled when my client asked for a dark upholstered bedroom. We selected a slubby chocolate-brown silk for the walls and a silk shag rug of the same color for the floor. This deep richness needs to be tempered with art and furnishings of lighter value. Here a Picasso painting and a racy Richard Prince collage are combined with a Nakashima bed and custom white-gilded bedside tables.

Plan

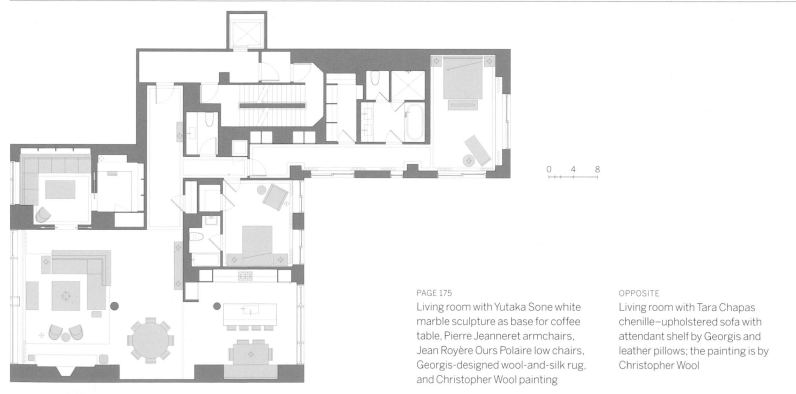

0   4   8

PAGE 175
Living room with Yutaka Sone white marble sculpture as base for coffee table, Pierre Jeanneret armchairs, Jean Royère Ours Polaire low chairs, Georgis-designed wool-and-silk rug, and Christopher Wool painting

OPPOSITE
Living room with Tara Chapas chenille–upholstered sofa with attendant shelf by Georgis and leather pillows; the painting is by Christopher Wool

IFYOUCAN
TTAKEAJO
KEYOUCAN
GETTHEFU
CKOUTOFM
YHOUSE

Breakfast room with George
Nakashima table, Richard Neutra
chairs, Serge Mouille sconce, Keith
Haring sculpture, and Christopher
Wool drawing

View from foyer toward dining room
with Jean-Michel Basquiat painting
and Jean Prouvé commode

Wenge-paneled library with suede
banquette and shearling pillows,
custom mirror-and-bronze coffee
table, and Alexander Calder
sculpture

Southampton Residence

Southampton, New York
2009

Shingle Style Redux. *Georgis designed this 8,600-square-foot, seven-bedroom contemporary version of a Shingle Style beach house in Southampton. Georgis was also responsible for the interior architectural finishes and millwork, but not the decoration. The design had to comply with environmental regulations to preserve wetlands and protect against flooding. The light and airy interior, unlike those of its rambling predecessors, extends in an open plan from a two-story stair/entry hall at the corner, which provides access to a sequence of public rooms around the swimming pool as well as to views toward Phillips Pond. Perpendicular to the main house and forming an entry forecourt is a wing housing a garage, game room, and guest and staff rooms. On the second floor, a double-loaded corridor leads to bedrooms, library, and playroom. Like those of the exterior, interior architectural details are contemporary, abstract interpretations of their Shingle Style models. Architectural finishes include oak floors and doors, a limestone fireplace, and Turkish white marble.*

Southampton Residence

My clients had a specific vision for this residence: a house grounded in the past but informed by the present—a hybrid of sorts. Vernacular architecture, developed over time, responds to local weather, light, and building materials. The vernacular tradition is especially rich on the east end of Long Island. From the seventeenth century on, farm buildings were framed and sheathed in locally sourced shingles and featured simple gable and gambrel roofs. The Shingle Style, developed from this tradition in the nineteenth century, assembled similar shapes and materials into picturesque and rambling compositions. In the 1960s and 1970s, architects like Norman Jaffe and Robert A. M. Stern appropriated the vocabulary of the Shingle Style for their modernist agendas. This project is similar in intent.

The house occupies a beautiful site on a former potato farm. Stringent local and federal restrictions defined setback requirements from the Atlantic Ocean, Phillips Pond, and Sayre Pond, making the site planning extremely challenging. In addition, Suffolk County Department of Health regulations demanded that the main floor of the building be set eight feet above the ground. I turned this constraint into an advantage: situating the house on a substantial berm afforded the opportunity for a grand twenty-four-foot-wide stair reminiscent of those by André Le Nôtre at Versailles and Vaux le Vicomte.

My answer to the clients' request is an austere interpretation of the Shingle Style. Traditional materials like shingles and a standing-seam metal roof are combined with more modern poured and exposed concrete to achieve a contemporary effect. The plan is configured to take advantage of views of all three bodies of water.

The entry sequence signals that this is not a traditional residence. Instead of aligning the front door with the grand entry stair, I located the main and service doors to either side of the axis of the wide stairway. As visitors approach, they can see straight through the glass window wall of the living room and out toward the landscape beyond. There is something kind of perverse about this disposition, but also something modest—it's not so deliberate, and it undermines the grandiosity of the stair. Visual clues, such as the large windows next to the principal entry, make clear which door is the main one.

The house is laid out with a conventional and gracious hierarchy. A raffia-paneled entry hall, with an adjacent mudroom, leads to a double-height stair hall containing a stairway made of plates of blackened steel. Next to the stair hall are a living room and a wing containing a family sitting room, bar, and powder room. The clients had requested that I omit a dedicated dining room—another aspect of the plan that undercuts the house's formality. The husband did not want a strict segregation of public rooms and service rooms, particularly since he enjoys cooking in a communal environment. So I developed a large dining space within the kitchen, creating a room that has become the heart of the house. All paths, corridors, and hallways lead to the kitchen, including a link to the wing that houses quarters for staff and guests.

The kitchen materials were specified to enhance its stature as a public space: cerused-oak cabinetry and paneling, white Italian porcelain floors, stainless-steel cabinetry and appliances, and crystallized glass counters give the room a rich, warm intimacy. The room is also blessed with fantastic views from the bay window to the swimming pool, idyllic Phillips Pond, and the dunes beyond. Upstairs, all bedrooms face the ocean; a cozy wood-paneled library with a vaulted ceiling overlooks Sayre Pond.

Plan, First Floor

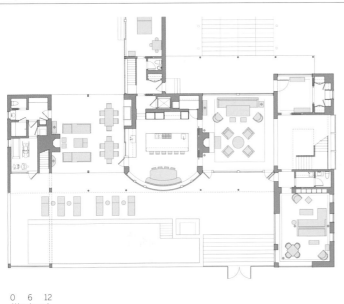

0   6   12

Plan, Second Floor

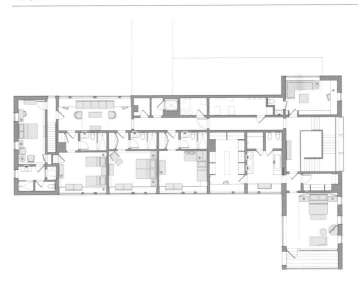

PAGE 183
Oceanside facade

OPPOSITE TOP
North and east facades

OPPOSITE, BOTTOM
Wide masonry stair leading to front entrance

Covered porch with view to Phillips
Pond and the Atlantic Ocean beyond

ABOVE
Pool deck with Valders limestone
paving; at the far end is a vertical
louvered screen

In this house I wanted to allude to Shingle Style detailing without re-creating it, to minimize and distill the essence of the vernacular in order to devise something relevant to the present. Casement windows, large picture windows, and sliding doors take the place of conventional doors and double-hung windows. Inside, V-grooved paneling replaces traditional beaded board. And doors with raised or recessed panels are reinterpreted as planes with single center panels that use V-groove boards rather than moldings and are flush with the frames.

TOP
Breakfast room with cerused-oak paneling, porcelain floors, glass-topped table, and island

ABOVE
Oak-paneled library

OPPOSITE
Stair hall with view to Sayre Pond

A Soho Address. *For this new condominium building in Soho, Georgis designed the public interiors and developed the floor plans, resulting in layouts that are a hybrid of hierarchically organized prewar rooms and open, loftlike spaces. He also designed the interiors of the apartments, including kitchens, bathrooms, and dressing rooms, using materials like rift- and quarter-sawn oak for the floors, statuary marble for the bathrooms, and American black walnut for the kitchen cabinets. Georgis decorated a three-bedroom model apartment with an eclectic mix of vintage and contemporary furnishings, as well as significant artworks from private collections. For the building's public entry sequence, including the lobby and elevator cab, Georgis collaborated with such artists as George Condo, Michele Oka Doner, and Peter Lane.*

Make It Fabulous

I had worked on multiple residential and commercial projects for this developer when he asked me to help him with a new condominium tower in Soho. My client had purchased the unbuilt project from another developer who had already gained city approval for the massing of the building. We could not alter the shape of the structure, only its exterior cladding and interiors.

I worked very closely with the developer and the architect who had designed the building envelope. I enjoy collaborating, whether with clients, artists, or other architects. In this case, the developer wanted very modern facades. I have reservations about floor-to-ceiling glass curtain walls, which have been overused in contemporary residential buildings. At ground level, glass walls foster a wonderful connection between interior and exterior, but above that, they induce vertigo. And I didn't want residents to feel as though they were living in a fishbowl. I introduced a wainscot at thirty inches high throughout the interior; this element offers a sense of enclosure and gives residents a blank surface to furnish against. On the exterior the wainscot is concealed behind glass spandrel panels.

The lobby and public spaces are discreet and welcoming. I created a suite of rooms paneled in dark-stained and cerused plain-sawn ash, paved in flinty Cold Spring granite, and detailed with bronze accents and white lacquered panels for contrast. These rooms seem closer in feeling to a private club than to a condominium lobby—I suppose the building is a club of sorts. Since Soho is a place where artists lived and made art, I paid homage to local history by commissioning artists for site-specific works. Michele Oka Doner, a longtime Soho inhabitant, made the entry door handles from bamboo cast in bronze; Peter Lane sculpted a ceramic screen; and George Condo made a painting for the lobby. A mélange of traditional and contemporary furnishings—a damask-covered wing chair, eighteenth-century French hall lantern, custom sofa, and purple-velvet-draped concierge desk—creates a timeless mix.

For the apartment interiors, the developer aspired to a composite of large open lofty public spaces and graciously planned private spaces—a mix of post- and prewar planning. Many condominiums completed in New York City around this time are overdesigned, often with four or five different materials in the kitchen alone. The bathrooms also seem contrived. Here we strove to create minimal, simple apartments of exceptional quality.

Another effort that differentiates our project from other developments is that the apartments are truly "decorator-ready." This is a term developers often use but rarely achieve. Because I have done a number of apartments within new buildings, I know the problems that are generally encountered. Residents pay too much for an apartment that requires them to then tear open walls to install audiovisual wiring and architectural lighting in the main spaces. On this project we hired a lighting designer and included architectural and decorative lighting in all spaces. Also, the apartments were prewired for audiovisual systems.

I traveled to Italy three times to select statuary white marble with gray veining for the bathrooms. In lieu of typical three-eighths-inch marble tile, we used marble slabs that ranged from three-quarters of an inch for the walls and floors to one and a quarter-inch for the countertops. The bathroom walls were preconstructed in Carrara to ensure that the marble was book-matched perfectly. The kitchens are finished with stainless steel, American black walnut, and Bethel white Vermont granite. Unlike many apartments in commercial developments, we made our floors from three-quarter-inch-thick rift- and quarter-sawn white oak. Two of the apartments have lushly planted gardens exceeding 1,300 square feet—like many of the features in this building, such gardens are a rarity in Manhattan.

Plan, Lobby

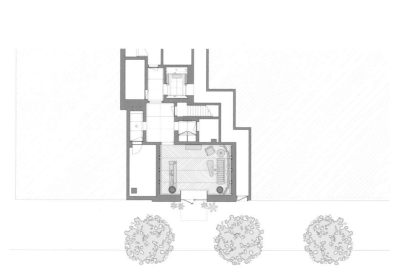

Plan, Third Floor

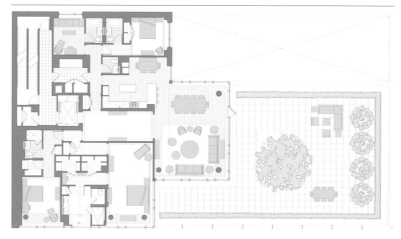

0 4 8

PAGE 191
Lobby with George Condo painting, Georgis-designed bronze-and-lacquer console, and damask-covered wing chair

ABOVE
Dining room and kitchen with
walnut table, Murano chandelier,
walnut-and-stainless-steel
cabinets, white granite counters,
oak floors, and Andy Warhol portrait

Make It Fabulous

BELOW
White-lacquered ribbon paneling, mohair-velvet concierge desk, and bronze-covered column with French bouillotte lamp in the lobby

RIGHT
Lobby with channel-tufted leather sofa by Georgis, vintage-glass-and-portoro-marble coffee tables, damask-covered wing chair, French hall lantern, and Peter Lane ceramic screen

Art House

*Apartment for Nelson Rockefeller, New York, 1937:
Interior design by Jean-Michel Frank with commissioned fireplace
mural by Fernand Léger*

William Georgis credits his partner, Richard D. Marshall, with introducing him to the world of contemporary art and artists. They met in 1989, when Marshall was a curator at the Whitney Museum of American Art, organizing exhibitions of postwar art. Now, Georgis says, "We live and breathe art. Richard is always curating exhibitions and art is integral to our lives." Art is also integral to Georgis's practice. Most if not all of his projects feature art as a major component of both the program and the decoration. He works with art in a variety of ways, whether incorporating existing or new collections into his interiors, collaborating with artists on the design of furnishings, or commissioning artists for site-specific pieces.

Many of Georgis's clients are already major collectors when they engage him. Then the challenge for Georgis is to design a place that showcases continually changing works of art. In some cases, clients ask for a neutral backdrop of white walls for a gallerylike installation. More often, Georgis sets up a dialogue between artworks, furnishings, and artifacts from different places and times. In his own townhouse, for instance, a seemingly casual Jack

Office suite in the Seagram Building, New York, 2010:
Polished and laser-cut stainless-steel sculpture with calligraphic texts by artist Mark Fox

Pierson sculpture spelling out "LOVER" hangs over a Venetian bed.

Georgis also enlists contemporary artists to design furnishings for his projects when he wants "to hear someone else's voice." Georgis frequently works with Nancy Lorenz, Michele Oka Doner, and Peter Lane, who straddle the worlds of fine, decorative, and applied arts, to create pieces that meet functional and aesthetic needs. Their furnishings add elements of handcraft into Georgis's rich mix of decoration, since these artists design and produce their works themselves. For an apartment on Fifth Avenue, for instance, Lorenz designed a wall of wood-and-gold-leaf panels to screen the closets in the master bedroom, at the same time providing a beautiful work of art. Oka Doner has worked with Georgis for decades, developing fixtures and furnishings from cast-bronze entry-door handles for a Soho apartment building to a sterling-silver top, titled *Celestial Pattern*, for a coffee table designed by Georgis. A ceramist and childhood friend from Oak Park, Lane has designed and made a variety of distinctive pieces, including sculptures based on sutra holders for Chinatown Brasserie, a ceramic screen for a Soho apartment building lobby, and tabletops, lamps, and planters for other venues.

In a similar vein, Georgis enriches projects with site-specific works by artists, often welcoming their solutions to complex design challenges. He takes a greater risk in these collaborations than he does with those for furnishings, turning over control of the

Fifth Avenue Apartment, New York, 2011: Vegetal imagery in the dining room, including Nancy Lorenz's water-gilded chrysanthemum tabletop on a lacquered tree-trunk base, hand-painted botanical china, and bark-textured silver

350 West Broadway, New York, 2010: Cast-bronze entry door handles designed by Michele Oka Doner

*Interior, 2008: Ossuary-themed powder room vestibule
designed by artist Virgil Marti*

*Fifth Avenue Apartment, New York, 2011: Gold-and-wood screen
designed by Nancy Lorenz to conceal bedroom closets*

content and design to the artist and limiting his role to setting the spatial parameters. The client for an apartment, for instance, proposed that Virgil Marti design a powder room. "I gave Marti the dimensions of the powder room and vestibule," Georgis says, "and I told him, 'Don't be respectful of me as an architect or designer. We really want you to go to town.' And he did." The result is a mirrored powder room decorated with églomisé spiderwebs and a vestibule-cum-ossuary ornamented with plaster florettes composed of skulls. For another project, the interior decoration of a large house, Georgis turned to the Brazilian Campana brothers, asking them "to design something to hang from the ceiling, to provide light, and to scale down the cavernous space." Their solution was a cumulus-cloud-like sculpture of wicker and lightbulbs that hovers in a large void, mitigating its size and creating an intimate sitting area below.

Marshall, now an independent curator and art adviser, has played an important role in integrating art into Georgis's projects. The architect notes that in a city like New York, where "art is the currency of the realm," Marshall often provides his clients with entrée to the world of contemporary art, introducing them to artists, educating new collectors, helping to install collections, and identifying and directing artists for site-specific commissions. One project where Georgis and Marshall collaborated was an office suite in Manhattan's Mies-designed Seagram Building. Georgis decorated the public spaces

and private office suite of the managing partner;
Marshall helped him form an art collection for
the office. Because the client didn't want walls
for art to block a glass conference room, Marshall
recommended several artists for the creation of a
porous and open site-specific sculpture installation.
The client selected Mark Fox, who developed the
design with few constraints besides location and
size. In keeping with Georgis's decorative theme of
precious metals and bodily fluids, Fox's sculpture is
made of laser-cut polished stainless steel. Scrimlike
in its delicacy, the sculpture features calligraphic
texts related to the space and location, such as the
latitude and longitude of the Seagram Building.
The sculpture's highly visible location, between the
reception area and the corridor it defines, creates
the illusion, Georgis says, of people disintegrating
and reflecting behind the sculpture like ghosts,
an extraordinary effect that could not have been
created with architecture.

The merging of art and design is perhaps best
expressed in the lobby of Lever House. The owner
has commissioned many projects from Georgis and
has worked closely with Marshall on assembling
and installing his own collection. When the building
renovation was completed, Marshall proposed that
the owner use the lobby for art exhibition rather
than for retail or commercial purposes. Since 2002
this concept has proven to be an amenity for tenants
and has made Lever House a destination for both
art aficionados and tour groups. Initially, Marshall

*17 State Street, New York, 2001:
Commissioned light sculpture by R. M. Fischer*

*Residence, 2009: Living area with travertine "egg" lamps by
Studio Angeletti, Sigmar Polke painting, and commissioned wicker-
and-lightbulb sculpture by the Campana brothers*

Lever House, New York, 2001:
Lobby with Richard Dupont installation

Georgis-Marshall Residence, La Jolla, 2011: Maquette
and completed installation of artist Kim MacConnel's murals
in the dining room

borrowed pieces by such artists as Alexander Calder and John Chamberlain. More recently, he has worked with the client to commission unique works of art that often relate to the building's architectural qualities, ultimately forming the Lever House Art Collection. The intent, according to Marshall, is to be advanced and inventive, to show works of different media and expression without being repetitive, and to present art made in the twenty-first century. "The art is not decorative nor is it easily digestible," Marshall says. "Even though it's viewable from the street, we don't shy away from nudity, sex, or politics." Whereas most of the "art houses" created by Georgis and Marshall are private, Lever House and its collection represent a very public dialogue between architecture and art.

D.A. and N.S.

Montana Residence

Big Sky, Montana
2010

The Wild West. *Located in the Rocky Mountains near Big Sky, Montana, the 13,600-acre Yellowstone Club provides a dramatic setting for this two-and-a-half-story, seven-bedroom, 7,300-square-foot log residence. The house is organized around a main entry/stair hall, with the public areas—a double-height great room and open kitchen/dining area—on one side and the bedrooms on the other. Upstairs are additional bedrooms, including the master suite, and a billiards area overlooking the great room. On the lowest level is a media room. A separate building, connected by an enclosed breezeway, houses the garage, with guest quarters above. Georgis's decoration looks to American West themes: a wall "veneer" of recycled, hand-chiseled half-logs enhances the rusticity of the great room; a custom moose-antler sofa is juxtaposed with a 1960s Laverne Lucite armchair, 1950s Italian sconces, and a stuffed bobcat lurking in the wood trusses of the great room. The house also features artwork by Louise Bourgeois, Doug Aitken, Richard Serra, and Joan Mitchell.*

Log construction has a long tradition in America, starting in the seventeenth century with Nya Sverige, or New Sweden, in the Delaware and Brandywine River Valleys, coming to an apogee in the nineteenth century with the construction of the Adirondack camps, and being revived at iconic national park hotels such as Old Faithful Inn at Yellowstone. Log houses are built to this day, often nostalgically evoking the era of settlement in the American West. In the case of this relatively new community, the developers and homeowners used log houses to create a place that enhanced the particularities of the locale. However, with appropriation of a historical style comes the danger of cliché. Ideally the historical style bears a trace of the time in which it was created and is also subject to transformation by a designer.

My clients, for whom I designed a Manhattan apartment, are sophisticated and well-traveled. When they bought this house from its original owners, they wanted to make small architectural changes and decorate it in a way that would avoid stereotype. Often when designing a space that already has strong architectural character, I reinforce the character with architecture while also working against it with furniture and other fittings. It is the introduction of the unexpected that encourages a dialogue between different cultures.

To develop the interior decoration scheme, I began with the conventions of the Wild West and went from there, refining the decorative tropes almost to the point of absurdity. For inspiration, I looked at Hollywood westerns and such atmospheric small-town thrillers as *Road House*. I looked at the great lodges of the National Park Service, where Asian elements were often used to brighten the dark interiors. I looked at the work of Thomas Canada Molesworth, the Wyoming-based designer who created furnishings for numerous ranches from the 1930s through the 1960s. The clients' contemporary art collection and vintage and custom furniture would introduce other notes into this somewhat somber house.

In the great room, a Western-lodge-like double-height space with a wooden truss ceiling and an enormous stone fireplace, I covered many of the sheetrock walls with recycled, milled log siding to make the interior even more rustic, and more atmospheric. This room was challenging to furnish because it has three focal points: the fireplace, a television to the right of the fireplace, and an enormous window with a spectacular view of the mountains. My strategy was to design a fourteen-foot daybed under the picture window so that a number of people could sit or recline to watch the television or take in the view; it also serves as a backdrop to a central seating arrangement. The daybed is covered in off-white Scottish cashmere and piled with pillows made from boiled wool, cashmere, and a faux-bois velvet. Birch-log armrests and legs, wrapped in white kidskin with enormous nailheads, complete the effect of luxe rusticity.

The great room, like the rest of the house, is furnished with a juxtaposition of Western Americana and other pieces: an antler wing sofa made in the style of Molesworth; green-velvet-covered Czechoslovakian wingback chairs from the 1950s; a rustic but high-style lacquer 1950s sofa table from Finland; French ceramic lamps. A Biedermeier stool is mixed with a nineteenth-century English oyster-veneered coffee table and a deer-hoof lamp with a plaid lampshade reminiscent of Hollywood westerns. A contemporary chandelier by Jeff Zimmerman resembles a grapevine, and Richard Serra's aggressive oil stick drawing stands up to the stone fireplace. A stuffed raccoon overlooks a chess table; a bobcat peers down from the trusses.

Other public areas that introduce the unexpected include the bar and the media room. I transformed what was a dull bar using upholstered zebra walls, black leather trim, nailheads, an Art Deco mirror, and tusks. It has a kind of 1930s French sensibility, but the zebra gives it a rustic quality. The media room, or man cave, has Siberian birch-bark walls inspired by the Art Deco smoking room in the French Embassy in Ottawa, Canada. This room contains an enormous bedlike sofa; visitors can sit and drink whisky and watch sports for hours on end. A bar with margarita and popcorn machines is the finishing touch.

Plan, Main Floor

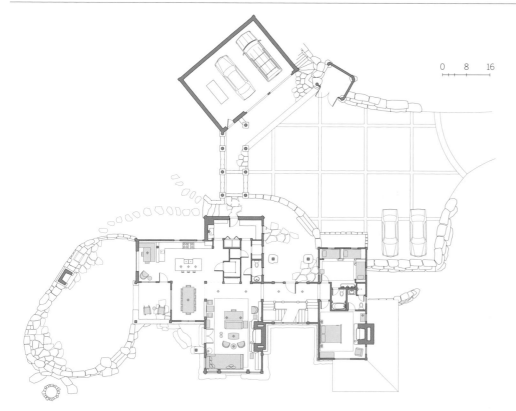

0   8   16

PAGE 202
View of great room from pool room balcony; a stuffed bobcat perches in the rafters

OPPOSITE
Great room with log siding, stone fireplace, Thomas Canada Molesworth–style sofa, English oyster-veneered coffee table, Czech modernist wingback chairs, hoof lamp, Biedermeier stool, Richard Serra drawing, and Jeff Zimmerman chandelier

ABOVE
Master bedroom with stone fireplace, Stilnovo chandelier, and fur-draped leather armchair

OPPOSITE
Media room with Siberian-birch-covered walls, sofa with shearling and leather pillows, and painting by Rose Wylie

Fifth Avenue Apartment
New York, New York
2011

Central Park Tree House. *This apartment, located in a mid-1920s residential building on the Upper East Side, was remodeled and decorated by Georgis as a two-bedroom residence for two "empty nesters." The main public rooms—living room, dining room, and library—of this 3,200-square-foot floor-through apartment overlook Fifth Avenue and Central Park. These rooms are entered from a central foyer and open onto each other with a flexible arrangement of pocket doors—the spaces can function as a suite or as individual rooms. The study and bedrooms, which face a residential side street, are separated from the kitchen and service facilities by gallerylike halls lined with artwork. Custom-designed furnishings by Georgis, as well as artists such as Nancy Lorenz and David Wiseman, are integrated with the clients' art collection, which includes works by George Condo, Mark Grotjahn, Jim Hodges, Grayson Perry, and Fred Tomaselli.*

Fifth Avenue Apartment

My aim in this apartment renovation was to open up as many rooms as possible to western light and views of Central Park. I started with the plan, organizing the rooms en suite, in the French manner, to frame views from one room to the next. The architectural concept is reinforced by the decorative scheme. The interior is a metaphor for a tree house, or an apartment in the trees, complete with vegetal imagery and allusions to nature.

The clients requested traditional architectural details, so I developed a language based on eighteenth-century French classicism seen through twenty-first-century eyes and serving twenty-first-century requirements for comfort. Custom decorative moldings, for instance, accommodate air conditioning: a lantern of fretwork in the foyer; a neoclassical cornice, abstract and contemporary in scale, in the living room; a cornice of fretwork in the dining room.

The clients also wanted to accommodate different scales of entertaining easily and comfortably. They had come from a much larger apartment, and they were accustomed to having space and furniture to host events large and small. Here, since there was less space, I had to engineer the rooms and furniture for double and triple duty. To confirm the flexibility of pieces and the workability of different arrangements, I made multiple mockups of furniture in cardboard, fussing over each inch—it was crucial that the size work correctly.

Two seating groups in the living room can work independently or together. One consists of an eighteen-foot-long "limousine sofa" with pull-up chairs that can accommodate two and even three clusters of guests. The second grouping, located by the Pavanazzo marble Louis XV mantle, is created from two nickel, resin, and shearling demi-chaises and a custom coffee table with a vitrine top containing Jim Hodges's gilded *Los Angeles Times* newspaper. Small book groups, family gatherings, or a concert for one hundred are accommodated equally well.

From the outset my clients wanted a bohemian living room— a room that people wouldn't want to leave—with an eclectic but elegant mix of furnishings. My first move was to splash color from Central Park across the floor in a custom rug woven by V'Soske. The limousine sofa, covered in silk velvet from the legendary French weaver Prelle, provides a backdrop for a monumental contemporary Joris Laarman coffee table carved from two blocks of Carrara marble, a pair of Dupré-Lafon slipper chairs, and two eighteenth-century Swedish Sulla chairs covered in a silk zebra print. I suppose it is fantastical to think zebras could roam Central Park *or* this apartment.

The formal dining room has been invaded by forest flora in the guise of a dining table by artist Nancy Lorenz that has a lacquered-tree-trunk base and a top featuring water-gilded chrysanthemums carved in low relief. Seed Pod dining chairs upholstered in dark green distressed leather and leaf-green velvet surround the luminous surface. A bower of bronze, porcelain, and crystal branches, leaves, and flowers by artist David Wiseman—a bower that emits light—takes the place of a traditional chandelier. In both living and dining rooms, I lined the window jambs with mirrors—an old trick that extends views. Hanging at each window is an overscaled mesh treillage scrim lit from above that glimmers at night.

The suite of public rooms also includes the library. Originally shut off from the rest of the apartment, the space has been opened to the foyer, to the living room, and to views of the park. Paneled in bleached anigre wood and furnished with a teddy-bear-mohair sofa and tiger-print silk rug, this room is the ultimate refuge.

Plan

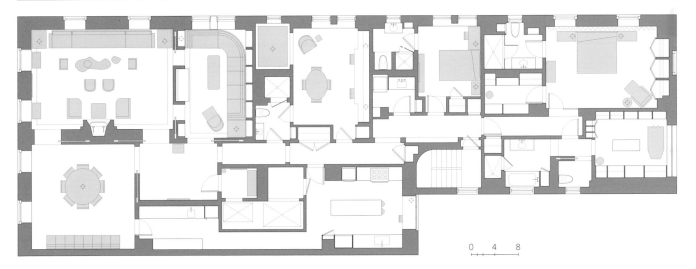

0   4   8

PAGE 212
Living room with eighteenth-century Louis XV Pavanazzo marble mantle; George Condo painting; and nickel, resin, cashmere, and shearling settees, nickel-and-glass vitrine coffee table, and Color Splatter silk-and-wool rug, all designed by Georgis

OPPOSITE
Anigre-paneled library with Jean Gillon lounge chair and ottoman; in the mica-clad foyer is a painting by George Condo

ABOVE
Office alcove with jaguar-patterned
silk mattress and Indian wall
hanging

Library with mohair sofa, velvet
pillows, Georgis-designed pen-shell
coffee table, tiger-patterned silk rug,
and Nathan Mabry busts

These clients love to entertain groups of all sizes. To accommodate the variety of events to be hosted here, I devised a dining table as flexible as a contortionist. It can be configured as one or two round tables six feet in diameter, a racetrack with leaves of thirteen feet, or two console tables. Such versatility allows the owners to host small intimate dinners or to clear the center of the room for large receptions.

ABOVE
Dining room with Nancy Lorenz chrysanthemum-patterned gold-leaf dining table, Georgis's velvet Seed Pod dining chairs, and salon-style installation of contemporary artworks

ABOVE
View from foyer to dining room with
Daniel Silver bust; in the dining room
is David Wiseman's illuminated
bower

ABOVE
George Condo sculpture in
living room

RIGHT
Living room with eighteenth-
century Swedish Sulla chairs in
zebra silk velvet, Paul Dupré-Lafon
slipper chairs, Joris Laarman
Cumulus marble coffee tables, and
Color Splatter rug by Georgis

LEFT
Master bedroom with silk-upholstered walls, bed and bedside tables designed by Georgis, rock crystal lamps, and Nancy Lorenz gold-and-wood screen

ABOVE
Leather-topped desk, Empire chair, and marbleized sliding doors in office

OPPOSITE AND ABOVE
Powder room with bullet-riddled
mirrors and Murano eyeball
pendant

*The clients deemed my proposals for the powder room "too tasteful" until
I suggested panels of bullet-shot mirrors. I can imagine an aging Joan
Crawford walking in, looking into the mirror, and pulling a mother-of-pearl-
handled pistol out of her clutch to obliterate the lies. When I asked my clients
if they were ready for shattered mirrors, they exclaimed, "Yes!" Guests have
asked, "My God—what happened in there?"*

La Jolla Akropolis. *This vacation house for Georgis and his partner, Richard D. Marshall, overlooks the La Jolla Bay. Located 350 feet above sea level on Mount Soledad, it was designed in 1955 by architect William Lumpkins as his own residence. The modernist house, with a hint of Japanese influence, situated on a ledge parallel to the steep slope, is one room deep, affording two exposures for most rooms. Christened the "Akropolis" (Georgis is of Greek origin), the three-thousand-square-foot, four-bedroom house was substantially rebuilt and converted to a two-bedroom house with a library and office. Through the demolition of an unsympathetic addition and the installation of a twenty-foot-high retaining wall, the architect reclaimed space behind the house for a pool and a suite of exterior garden rooms. Judy Kameon designed the landscape.*

As Richard and I were searching for vacation houses in La Jolla, we happened upon a modernist gem designed by the architect Russell Forester. The disciplined, minimal, almost severe house was being sold by the estate of the original owners. The interiors contained modern furnishings and, more surprisingly, some nineteenth-century pieces. The only inhabitant was the owners' cat, which sat on an antique French chair upholstered in needlepoint (completed, I liked to think, by the lady of the house). The effect was mesmerizing. The decor spoke to the idea of migration, Manifest Destiny, and settlers transporting their prized possessions across the continent via covered wagon—and also a desire to inhabit a modern setting. The mixture of the old with the new perhaps gave the owners a sense of security in a foreign place.

This was our story also. Although Richard and I had both spent time earlier in our lives in California, we were migrating west in search of something new. We wanted a modern house, but we also had a New York storeroom full of furnishings and art—in short, we had baggage.

We ended up buying a different modernist house, one designed by the architect and painter William Lumpkins. It had fallen into disrepair by the time we purchased it, and it required substantial reimagining and structural retrofitting. On the lower level I maintained the entry foyer and converted the adjacent garage into a guest suite. The upper level required more substantial intervention. I reconfigured an enfilade of three bedrooms and two and a half baths into an eight-room suite: an upper-level foyer, dining room, kitchen, living room, library, office, master bedroom, and one and a half baths. A new steel structural system supports a cantilevered terrace off the living room and raised ceilings in the dining room and library. All spaces enjoy spectacular views of the Pacific Ocean; most also have views and access to the garden behind. The garden was developed as a series of exterior rooms that expand and relate specifically to the adjacent interior areas.

Mirroring a garden foyer is the upper-level foyer, where I restored a decorative wood screen and covered the walls in brown grass cloth. This material was popular at the time the house was built, in both America and Asia. Artist Barbara Kruger created *BE HERE NOW* specifically for the space.

The living room takes its cues from the Orient. Given the view east, why not gild the Japanese-style irimoya ceiling in the manner of a Kyoto temple? I used Japanese-made tea paper to reflect light bouncing off the Pacific Ocean and the rear swimming pool. A black-and-white ink stain carpet I designed is a vibrant foundation for a suite of nineteenth-century Danish Egyptian Revival furniture acquired years ago at auction, a pair of Art Deco settees, an Eastlake chair, and a Fred Brouard coffee table. A nineteenth-century German Grand Tour painting of the ruins of Agrigento, an ancient Greek colony that is now part of Sicily, refers to the house's terrain and namesake, while ants swarm the wood-grain paper of Ed Ruscha's prints. The mix is forged of pieces from our past and the genius loci.

Directly adjacent to the living room, wedged between the house and the slope of Mount Soledad, is a swimming pool. Limestone stepping stones lead through the pool to the other side of the garden and accentuate the position of the living room, serendipitously bookended by two bodies of blue water.

Dark rooms in Mediterranean climates offer a particularly alluring refuge. The library, inspired by wooden cigar boxes, is paneled in olive-brown stained and cerused ash. A curved mirror-topped bar, reminiscent of those seen in old Hollywood movies, is fully stocked with

Plans, Lower and Main Floors

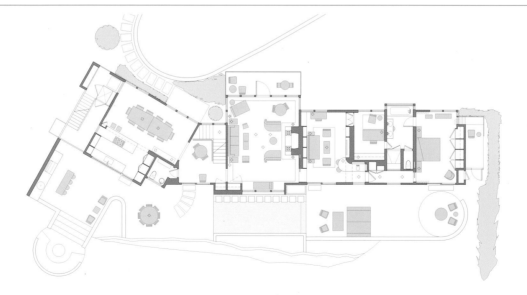

0   6   12

PAGE 227
La Jolla Bay facade

OPPOSITE
Cerused-ash-paneled bar with bronze-mirror counter and vintage Mexican silver; in the master bedroom beyond are an Alex Katz painting and Karpen of California's Horn chair

In the days of the China trade, gilded papers were put in the tops of tea boxes made for export. The English glued the metallic squares to walls, giving them a luminous, reflective quality, and started a trend that continues intermittently to this day. To me this is a brilliant example of recycling in the service of decor.

ABOVE
Living room with nineteenth-century Danish Egyptian Revival sofa, cast-glass-and-steel coffee tables and Ink Splatter rug by Georgis, and nineteenth-century painting of Agrigento

RIGHT
Tea-papered ceiling, Georgis-designed Murano lanterns, Art Deco loveseats, Fred Brouard coffee table, and Mike Kelley drawing in the living room

Guest suite with Billy Haines coffee table, sofa with antique-Japanese-textile pillows, Burdick glass-and-aluminum desk, and installation of contemporary drawings and photographs

LEFT
Library with cerused-ash paneling,
Jean Royère armchairs, shearling-
and-Fortuny sofa, English-leather-
book side tables, Murano parrot
lamps, and George Condo painting

ABOVE
Ned Smyth mosaic-and-concrete
palm tree sculpture, Dorothy
Schindele desk, and Paul McCobb
chair in library

ABOVE
Outdoor dining area with view to
outdoor kitchen and grotto with
aloe, banana tree, and succulents

LEFT
Poolside double chaise with view to
fire pit and Sol Bloom chairs with
pindo palm and pittosporum hedge

ABOVE
Outdoor dining area, Norman Foster
glass-topped table, and lap pool with
stepping stones

ABOVE
Master bath with driftwood-
finished cedar, unfilled travertine
vanity and floor, Fontana Arte
sconces, and Seguso shell
soap dish

RIGHT
Master bedroom with Horn chair,
seventeenth-century Coromandel
screen, and Hermès stool

OVERLEAF
View into living room with
nineteenth-century French ceramic
sphinxes and Sol Bloom chairs; the
balcony looks over the La Jolla Bay

Acknowledgments

I am extraordinarily grateful to all who participated in the making of this monograph and in the making of the work. Donald Albrecht and Natalie Shivers, dear friends and esteemed colleagues, created the structure for this book and wrote insightful texts. Without Gianfranco Monacelli's imprimatur, this volume would not be possible. Andrea Monfried patiently shepherded the authors, proffering superb guidance and incisive editing. Elizabeth White saw to the exceptional quality of illustrations and to the overall production of the book. Paul Carlos of Pure+Applied brought his visual acuity to the design of this book. T. Whitney Cox went beyond the call of his photographic duties in support of this volume. Karen Diaz looked after innumerable details large and small. Richard D. Marshall and Karen D. Stein were generous in reviewing texts and graphic presentation. Joyce Louie, William McBarron, and Ilya Mirgorodsky, along with others in my office, have been invaluable and inspired colleagues and collaborators. Many thanks to Aby J. Rosen, Samantha Boardman Rosen, Christopher J. Carrera, Emily Chen, Harvey M. Schwartz, Anne Hubbard, Liz Rosen, Nora Kohen, Alfredo Ghirardo, Andreas and Katerina Dracopoulos, and all my patrons and friends, who are fellow believers that heaven is attainable on earth. They have spread the gospel.

Project Credits

Park Avenue Apartment, New York, New York, 1998
Architect-in-Charge: William T. Georgis
Assistant Architect: Silvina Goefron
Interior Designer: William T. Georgis
Lighting Designer: Johnson Schwinghammer Lighting Consultants

Park Avenue Apartment, New York, New York, 2004
Architect-in-Charge: Ilya Mirgorodsky
Interior Design Associate: Joyce Louie
Interior Design Assistant: Heather Ba

Lever House, New York, New York, 2001
Architect-in-Charge: Eun Sun Chun
Assistant Architect: Gustavo Penengo
Interior Design Associate: Joyce Louie
Associate Architect: Skidmore, Owings & Merrill
Landscape Architect: Workshop: Ken Smith Landscape Architect
Lighting Designer: Johnson Schwinghammer Lighting Consultants

Georgis-Marshall Townhouse, New York, New York, 2001
Architect-in-Charge: Sik Lam
Assistant Architects: Eun Sun Chun, Edward H. A. Tuck
Interior Design Associate: Joyce Louie
Interior Design Assistant: Heather Ba
Landscape Contractor: The Window Box
Structural Engineer: John D. Nakrosis Jr.
MEP Engineer: Tri-Power Engineering
Lighting Designer: Davis Mackiernan Architectural Lighting

Apartment at the Carlyle Hotel, New York, New York, 2001
Architect-in-Charge: William T. Georgis
Assistant Architect: Jorge Porta
Interior Design Associate: Joyce Louie
Structural Engineer: Hanington Engineering Consultants
MEP Engineer: Hanington Engineering Consultants
Lighting Designer: Davis Mackiernan Architectural Lighting

Park Avenue Penthouse, New York, New York, 2003
Architect-in-Charge: William McBarron
Assistant Architect: Ilya Mirgorodsky
Interior Design Associate: Joyce Louie
Interior Design Assistant: Ann Mairi Dagayday
Landscape Architect: Edmund Hollander Design
Structural Engineer: Gilsanz Murray Steficek
MEP Engineer: Hanington Engineering Consultants
Lighting Designer: Davis Mackiernan Architectural Lighting

Beach House, Southampton, New York, 2003, 2012
Architect-in-Charge: William McBarron
Assistant Architects: Eun Sun Chun, Michelle Frankel,
Ron Millett, Ilya Mirgorodsky
Interior Design Associate: Joyce Louie
Interior Design Assistant: Heather Ba
Landscape Architect: Nievera Williams Design
Structural Engineer: Hanington Engineering Consultants (2003),
Steven L. Maresca (2012)
MEP Engineer: Hanington Engineering Consultants

East Side Townhouse, New York, New York, 2004
Architect-in-Charge: William McBarron, Ilya Mirgorodsky
Assistant Architects: Eun Sun Chun, Ron Millett
Interior Design Associate: Joyce Louie
Interior Design Assistants: Ann Mairi Dagayday, Gabriella Lutz
Landscape Contractor: The Window Box
Structural Engineer: Hanington Engineering Consultants
MEP Engineer: Hanington Engineering Consultants
Lighting Designer: Davis Mackiernan Architectural Lighting

Summer Residence, Watermill, New York, 2005
Architects-in-Charge: William McBarron, Ilya Mirgorodsky
Assistant Architect: Ron Millet
Interior Design Associate: Joyce Louie
Interior Design Assistants: Ann Mairi Dagayday, Gabriella Lutz
Landscape Architect: Paula Hayes
Structural Engineer: Hanington Engineering Consultants
MEP Engineer: Hanington Engineering Consultants

Chinatown Brasserie, New York, New York, 2006
Architect-in-Charge: Ilya Mirgorodsky
Assistant Architect: Ron Millett
Interior Design Associate: Joyce Louie
Interior Design Assistant: Ann Mairi Dagayday
Lighting Designer: Davis Mackiernan Architectural Lighting

Palm Beach Apartment, Palm Beach, Florida, 2006
Architect-in-Charge: Ilya Mirgorodsky
Interior Design Associate: Joyce Louie
Interior Design Assistant: Ann Mairi Dagayday

East Quogue Residence, East Quogue, New York, 2007
Architect-in-Charge: Ilya Mirgorodsky
Assistant Architect: William McBarron
Interior Design Associate: Joyce Louie
Landscape Architect: Paula Hayes
Structural Engineer: Steven L. Maresca
Lighting Designer: Davis Mackiernan Architectural Lighting

Soho Apartment, New York, New York, 2008
Architect-in-Charge: Ilya Mirgorodsky
Assistant Architect: Ron Millett
Interior Designer: Tina Glavan
Building Architect: Ateliers Jean Nouvel

Gramercy Park Apartment, New York, New York, 2008
Architect-in-Charge: Ron Millett
Interior Designer: Tina Glavan
Building Architect: John Pawson

Southampton Residence, Southampton, New York, 2009
Architects-in-Charge: Ilya Mirgorodsky, William McBarron
Assistant Architect: Ron Millett
Interior Designer: David Kleinberg Design Associates
Landscape Architect: Perry Guillot
Structural Engineer: Steve L. Maresca
MEP Engineer: Hanington Engineering Consultants

350 West Broadway, New York, New York, 2010
Architect-in-Charge: Ron Millett
Interior Design Associate: Joyce Louie
Interior Design Assistant: Ann Mairi Dagayday
Building Envelope Architect: Moed de Armas & Shannon Architects
Architect of Record: SLCE Architects
Structural Engineer: WSP Flack and Kurtz
Lighting Designer: Davis Mackiernan Architectural Lighting

Montana Residence, Big Sky, Montana, 2010
Architect-in-Charge: William T. Georgis
Interior Designer: Tina Glavan
Interior Design Assistant: Angela Montoya

Fifth Avenue Apartment, New York, New York, 2011
Architects-in-Charge: Ilya Mirgorodsky, William McBarron
Assistant Architect: Robert Louis Benson III
Interior Design Associate: Joyce Louie
Interior Design Assistant: Ann Mairi Dagayday
Structural Designer: Hanington Engineering Consultants
MEP Engineer: Hanington Engineering Consultants
Lighting Designer: Davis Mackiernan Architectural Lighting

Georgis-Marshall Residence, La Jolla, California, 2011
Architect-in-Charge: Ilya Mirgorodsky
Assistant Architects: Robert Louis Benson III, Ron Millett
Interior Designer: Ann Mairi Dagayday
Landscape Designer: Elysian Landscapes

Illustration Credits

Unless noted below, all photographs are by T. Whitney Cox.
Numbers refer to page numbers.

Peter Aaron, Courtesy of Otto Archive: 14
William Abronowicz: 51, 73, 75, 76, 77, 78, 79, 80, 81, 82, 83
Jamie Ardiles-Arce: 169
The Art Institute of Chicago: Mrs. James Ward Thorne, *French Library of the Modern Period,* 1930s, c. 1937, mixed media: 8
Roberto D'Addona: 16 bottom, 85, 87, 121, 123, 124, 125, 126
Jesse David Harris: 201 top
William T. Georgis: 129 middle, 134 bottom, 135 bottom right
Getty Images: 135094331 (RM): 16 top; 56459325 (RM): 49
Getty Research Institute, Photography Archive, Los Angeles, California, photography by Julius Shulman: 127
Andre Mellone: 88 top, 89 top
Metropolitan Museum of Art/European Sculpture and Decorative Arts (43, 196): *Boiserie From the Hôtel de Cabris,* ca. 1774, with later additions; oak and plaster, painted and gilded; bronze-gilt, mirror glass, oak flooring, etc.: 9
Photofest: 84
Courtesy of Rockefeller Archive: 196 top
William Waldron: 44, 46, 47
Paul Warchol: 38, 43, 58, 59, 61